I Just Love My

QUARTO **Q** CONSULTING

I just
LOVE
my job!

**The 7P Way to a job you love
based on who you are**

**Roy Calvert
Brian Durkin
Eugenio Grandi
Kevin Martin**

Also by Quarto Consulting Ltd
First Find Your Hilltop

How to order: single copies may be ordered online at www.novavistapub.com.
To phone Nova Vista Publishing, dial +32-14-21-11-21.

Distributed to the book trade in the U.S. and Canada by National Book Network (+1-800-462-6420).

ISBN 90-77256-02-4

D/2003/9797/2

Printed and bound in Belgium.

20 19 18 17 16 15 14 13 12 11 10 9 8 7 6 5 4 3 2

Cover design: Bright Art Design
Text design: Layout Sticker

Contents

Part I: Putting Things In Perspective

Introduction 7
1 Your Hilltop - Your Unique World View 14
2 What Drives You? Basic 7P™ Types............................... 26
3 The Three Level Technique (3LT), Listening and Questioning 35

Part II: Drives, the 7Ps™ and Your Drive Profile

4 The 7Ps™ of Drive 42
5 The Product Drive.. 45
6 The People Drive... 61
7 The Process Drive 74
8 The Power Drive 87
9 The Plans Drive 103
10 The Positioning Drive 116
11 The Purpose Drive 131

Part III: Working Toward Change

12 Developing Your Unique Drives Profile.......................... 143
13 Making Changes – Vision to Action............................. 152
14 Change Through Communication – Influencing Others 164
15 Changing Jobs and Careers 173
16 Change Through Personal Development 179

Afterword 186
Quarto Consulting Notes 187
Index 188

PART 1

PUTTING THINGS
IN PERSPECTIVE

Introduction

*'I have so much to give in my work! I just want to be able to make my contribution – put some of **me** into the work I do. . . .'*

This comment, from a new entrant to the world of work, is typical of the enthusiasm and frustration of many people in the early days of their careers. But many of us feel the same frustration – our jobs don't tap our talents or fulfil our drives. In the last few years, a lot of management literature has focused on tapping the creative potential that lies within people in all of our organisations. Yet many employers have lost the resources of loyal, committed and undoubtedly creative people by not recognising and harnessing that potential.

This is a book about how *you* can influence your working life and develop *for yourself* situations that reward and nourish you. It is a book for the countless thousands of talented people who want to take more control over the work they do, whether they be ambitious young executives, mid-life career changers or simply those who feel that working for an organisation could – and should – fulfil them more than it presently does. *We firmly believe every person should be able to say, 'I just love my job!'*

These days, most of us expect that we will have a number of employers during our working life. This new pattern, and other changes in our work environment, have made it critically important for people to take individual responsibility for their own personal development. Organisations still support and encourage the development of their people. But unfortunately, many cannot offer the structured stages of job progression that used to take care of employees from their hiring day until their retirement.

As mergers and restructuring become the norm, there's much more fluidity in the movement of workers between organisations. There is also a bewildering proliferation of rapid change within many organisations. In this fluid, changeable environment, the opportunity for role and responsibility change has never been greater. People who clearly understand their own needs and drivers will be better placed to choose or shape roles, or to influence their areas of responsibility, in ways that suit them best.

You may have found this book while browsing in a book shop, looking for some new insights in self-development or career management. It may be that your manager has handed you this book, or it has been recommended by your HR department, perhaps leading you to ask, 'What's in it for my company?' As part of this self-development process, organisations benefit greatly. True, some lose good people to more enlightened companies or to self-employment, but others reap the rewards of a motivated workforce that is gaining intrinsic satisfaction from the work it does.

The issue, for us, is whether the initiative for developing human resources comes 'top down' or 'bottom up'. Many of the initiatives we have seen have failed through top down strategies. As Naisbitt said in *Megatrends*, fads are imposed from the top down, trends grow from the bottom up.

Trends are very powerful because they start slowly — 'bottom up' — and develop a momentum that becomes unstoppable until, when a critical mass is reached, they become the order of the day. Consider the current greening of society. Few of us, a decade ago, could predict the way that recycling, energy credits, global warming, holistic health and other trends have become mainstream drivers for policy and action. The grass-root concerns built from the bottom up.

The same is happening right now within organisations — a steady growth in the number of individuals who recognise that if they are to spend the majority of their waking life engaged in some kind of work activity, then that activity needs to fulfil them more than a pay cheque ever can. The time has never been riper for this change to gather speed.

It is now well-known that in recent years, we have moved into a period of severe skill shortages in many important sectors. Demographic changes have meant that fewer 16-year-olds as a percentage of the total population have been entering the labour pool. Employment for the under-30s has turned into a seller's market for people who have the right skills. The annual university and college recruitment drive for students has turned upside down in some sectors, with *students* interviewing *companies* rather than the other way round. A quick glance at the 'situations vacant' section in your newspaper demonstrates the degree to which the world of work has changed in recent years. The job titles now advertised were not on the lists of the school and college career advisors who counselled today's potential candidates for these roles.

One of the major issues for organisations has been how to attract and retain competent staff. Many forward-looking organisations have developed ranges of benefits to mitigate against talent losses: setting up crèche and playgroup facilities for the children of employees, calling on the over-50s to come back to work, offering bounty-hunter payments for employees who attract friends to work for their organisation. Some are laying the foundations of Employee Development Programmes that go far wider than the needs of the job to encompass University degree courses, vocational Professional Qualifications, fitness and leisure pursuits. It is not uncommon for organisations to have a catalogue of benefits which employees pick from, with packages that are designed to appeal to individuals with different lifestyles and values. Organisations that have improved their benefits and polices to better meet the needs of their employees report significant decreases in staff turnover, plus savings in recruitment costs.

Tom Peters and many others consider the Nineties to be a revolutionary decade, and that was before the common use of the Internet and web technologies. In fact, we are in the midst of the most dramatic changes in basic business organisation in over 2,000 years. There have been casualties: some organisations have gone under, some have merged or been taken over. Some jobs have changed or disappeared, and employees in many sectors who had once anticipated a stable career progression have found unexpected diversions. This change has been accelerated by the enormous increase in individually variable employment contracts and by the disappearance of the company pension, especially as this trend spreads into the public sector.

The trends and changes in 'work' have brought opportunities or problems, depending on how you view them. For those who know what they want and what they have to offer, the opportunities of this fluid work environment have been genuinely rewarding. The changing work environment continues and the portfolio career has become more commonplace. For those looking to *create or shape*, rather than *follow*, their career paths, the variety, fluidity and opportunity have never been so great.

The purpose of this book

This book will help you to know who you are, where you want to be, and how you get there. It will enable you to understand your predominant drives and motivations and how these shape your life and approach to work. It will enable you to understand your strengths and limitations and give you greater choice and control over your careers.

It is a book about understanding ourselves, learning why we do what we do, identifying the needs we have and seeing how we try to fulfil them. It is also a book about understanding others.

Throughout the book, we will be constantly crossing the boundaries between understanding ourselves and understanding others. There are two important reasons for this. The first is that we believe you cannot understand yourself without understanding others and vice versa. The second is that if you want to make changes in your job, your career or your whole life, this usually involves communicating with others to achieve those changes.

Most of our working lives involve us with people: we get what we want through interacting with our managers, staff, peers, customers, clients, etc. Very few people are in a position of splendid isolation: dealing with people is the business that most of us are in. The ability to communicate effectively is probably the single most powerful attribute in achieving our ends. This fact has never been truer as a matrix approach to organisational structure becomes more widespread. Traditional structures have become less important. Thus there is a greater reliance on people's ability to build and maintain relationships, working collaboratively to make things happen.

Making sense of how both we and others see the world is the basis of our approach to communication.

Personal awareness

In our work within organisations over the last two decades we have become acutely aware of a crucial gap in the focus of most training. Employees are given knowledge-based training on the particular specialisms of their role: product knowledge, procedures, etc. Many receive skills training in the form of management or personal skills development, e.g. interviewing, negotiating, managing teams, selling, and so on. The gap we find in virtually all the development courses we have experienced is in the arena of *personal awareness*.

People acquire the knowledge and skills to make them more effective like the components of a toolbox — a hammer for this task, a chisel for that, etc. Yet little emphasis seems to be placed on understanding the person wielding the tools, how they use them, their style of working, why they approach things in a certain way.

For people to grow their abilities, and become more effective in what they do, they need not only knowledge and skills but an awareness of themselves. Perhaps the taboo against finding out what we are really like or how others perceive us is fostered by a fear of personality assassination: feedback is perhaps seen as a polite word for criticism, judgment or blame.

That is not our position. A mirror in itself does not judge, it only reflects what is there. What each one of us does with reflections of ourselves is something only we can decide, and we are often our own worst critics. Yet without the reflections, without feedback, it is very difficult for us to see the backs of our own heads, to see ourselves as others see us.

Self-discovery

It is possible to develop personal awareness using the techniques in this book, plus feedback from colleagues and friends, without judgment. Learning about our drives, our predominant style, our strengths and our limitations need not be a sombre affair.

We invite you to take a journey of self-discovery, a journey that will take you through the parts of your inner world that dominate the way you operate. Let us quickly say that we are not attempting to involve you in a deeply psychoanalytic introspection. Neither are we claiming to deal with the whole complex nature of personality. The circumstances of your childhood might be an interesting topic for discussion with your therapist, but that is not the route we wish to take.

Our focus will be in the areas of needs, drives, motivation and style. We believe that, working with these elements, it is possible to develop an awareness of how they dictate your approach to life and the work you do, without having to fully understand what in your formative years may have caused them. We are not in any way devaluing the splendid work of many therapists, merely acknowledging our distinct route through a very complex area.

On any journey we need a map, whether it is one that is written down in some form or etched into our memories through familiarity. A map is an attempt to represent reality in an abstract form. We have maps for everything, not just for travelling. Concepts are mental maps that allow us to describe things to each other or to predict things in our world.

Some maps are of course better than others — better in terms of being more accurate, more detailed, more useful in the way they represent the terrain, etc. The challenge for us has been in developing a map that strikes a balance between the complexities of theoretical elegance on one hand and the superficiality of the pop magazine questionnaire on the other.

The map we have developed as a means of charting our route is based on the premise that a map should be practically useful, that it should relate to real world experience for many readers and that it should have a high degree of predictiveness – that is, that one should be able to predict a lot about someone's behaviour from knowing a little.

We have developed this map or framework — we call it the 7P™ model — out of years of working with individuals and groups in a wide range of organisational settings and cultures. We have taught this model, or appropriate parts of it, to thousands of individuals to enable them to be more effective in the work they do: managers who need to understand how to relate better to their staff, graduate trainees who want to plan an appropriate induction route, consultants who need to get closer to their clients, team members who want to assess collective strengths and limitations. Throughout our work, whether we are imparting technical knowledge on project implementation or teaching specific skills such as influencing, a major focus is always on developing awareness of the individual's drives and style and how these can expand or limit the work he or she does.

How to use this book

This book is designed not only to be read but also to be worked with. It is one thing to study a map in detail sitting indoors. It is quite another to take it with you to explore the territory it relates to. There are some people who will merely read this book to gain an appreciation of the concepts within it. For others, who want to explore the territory, and to understand how the 7P model relates to their own inner terrain, we have included short exercises in each section and offer a technique that can be used as a self-discovery tool.

In Part I, you will find an introduction to the basic concepts of hilltops, drives, the 7Ps of drive, drive profiles, and the Three Level Technique (3LT).
- Hilltops is a metaphor for each person's unique perspective on the world, informed by what he or she values, strives for and considers important.
- Drives energise your behaviour and give it direction.
- The 7Ps help differentiate among drives, relating to Purpose, Position, Plans, Power, Process, People and Product.
- The Three Level Technique (3LT) helps you discover not just what people do or how they do it, but why – so you can really understand them, and also understand yourself, more deeply.

Part II takes you through each of the 7P drives in detail. You will learn each drive's characteristics and begin to chart your own profile of each drive's relative strength in your own makeup.

Part III puts it all together, and gives you the Vision to Action process model. It helps you make change happen by committing to it and then by learning to influence others so they support the changes you need to make.

Taken together, the insights, tools, processes and concepts in this book will give you what you need for greater satisfaction in your work life, and beyond.

For those of you who are prepared to commit some energy to understanding yourself, we believe the rewards are great, for with personal awareness comes choice. By understanding clearly what drives us – why we do what we do – we open up the possibility of choosing other ways of fulfilling our needs. If we understand how we relate to other people and how we may be predictably perceived by them, we open up the possibility of communicating in different ways and increasing the likelihood of getting our needs met.

The approach we use is more than a self-reflection device. It can be used equally well to explore, understand and appreciate the motivations and drives of others, to gain some insight into who you have as a colleague, boss, customer etc., and therefore how best to communicate with him or her.

Although the focus of the book is specifically on business and the world of work, all of us are also in the business of life. We will be drawing on examples from the breadth of society, from the media, sport, politics and relationships of many kinds to enrich the ideas we present. It is relevant to recognise that for many of us our leisure pursuits are often the means by which we fulfil those drives that work does not satisfy. To limit understanding of ourselves to only a business context would increase the potential of seeing ourselves as somewhat flat, two-dimensional creatures, stifled by our office attire.

Almost above all, we hope this book will be fun to read and work with rather than a 'sober manual for the earnest enquirer'. In such a business book we may run the risk of sounding somewhat unprofessional, yet over and over again we find that learning increases enormously when there is enjoyment in the activity. Learning about oneself should be fun! We suspect that those of us who find it difficult to laugh at ourselves are the people who least accept who we are, and who will be the ones who find it the most difficult to change.

So we invite you to start this exploration and learning process with an open mind and a playful attitude. With that approach, plus your own commitment, we feel confident you can come to say, 'I just love my job!' with pleasure and conviction. Good luck!

Quarto Consulting Ltd

Roy Calvert   Brian Durkin   Eugenio Grandi   Kevin Martin

CHAPTER 1

Your Hilltop –
Your Unique World View

'All the world's queer except me an' thee, lad, an' even thee's a bit queer at times!'
Old Yorkshire saying

Do you find some people strange? How often do you hear people say, 'I just don't understand what goes on inside his head!' or 'What on earth is she up to?' or 'I can't fathom him out at all'. Making sense of people is enormously complex and can involve many difficulties. Over many years we have observed a spectrum of responses to the task. For some, human behaviour is a totally fascinating area and they get deeply immersed in understanding why we do what we do. Others, faced with the possibility that we may never understand, simply give up trying.

By facing up to this challenge we hope to produce a way of understanding people that is realistic and useful, and which is rich enough to make sense of some of the living complexity we find.

Do you ever stop to consider how very different people are? As you go about your daily work, do you ever contemplate what a diverse bunch of people it is that you meet? Think about your colleagues, your managers or staff, your customers, or people in other departments in your organisation. Do you know what makes them tick? When you are trying to work with them, selling or negotiating, managing or persuading them, do you know how to handle them, what will work with different individuals?

Think of the thousands of different jobs in our society, and the kinds of skills and qualities that are needed for each. There are people with ability all around the world searching for, and thankfully in some cases, finding, niches in life that they find rewarding.

What are the skills and qualities you bring to your job? Do you feel that your job uses your abilities to their best advantage, or are you constantly coping with frustration? What rewards do you get from doing the work you do?

There is an old and well-known saying that goes, *'If you want to be happy, find something you love doing so much that you would do it for free - then do it so well that people will pay you to do it for them!'* If you are able to say with your hand on your heart that the work you do satisfies this criterion, then give this book to someone less fortunate than yourself. If not, we need to begin some self-exploration to unearth what it is that you love, what rewards you seek, and what mixture of skills and qualities you have.

For many people, finding out what they really want to do is the major obstacle. It is easy to be earmarked for a particular career because you display abilities in that area, and even easier to drift into a line of work that pays well – only to become dissatisfied. So we need to start at the basis of what makes *you* a unique being, what *you* value and strive for in your own world, the things that you consider to be important in life.

We have all grown up in an age of ever-increasing exposure to the media. The global windows of television and the Internet allow access into people's lives that simply was not possible a couple of decades ago. From interviews with corporate executives in Japan to remote tribes threatened with extinction in the rain forests of Brazil to chat rooms on countless topics, television and the Internet offer the opportunity to glimpse something of the inner needs of the eccentric and the ordinary, the powerful and powerless. And yet, for every life we glimpse, there are millions who remain invisible.

When we look at the fragment of humanity that we have access to – whether through the porthole of the media or through personal contact – we are constantly impressed by seeing people going to amazing lengths to satisfy some need or other. What drives them? Why do people do what they do? What is it, for instance, that drives a person to devote the whole of his or her life to the service of others in the slums of the third world? What drives someone to surf a fifty-foot Pacific wave on eight feet of fibre-glass when a mistake would cost all?

What drives someone to spend most of their adult waking life satisfying the need to collect things, be it butterflies or businesses, constantly gathering more, bigger, better? We have worked with groups of professionals, each one annually earning the equivalent of £300,000 plus, who admitted that their typical working day was still 14 to 16 hours, six days a week! Why?

What drives someone to spend their life peering down a microscope in a laboratory, or studying theoretical physics or Chaos theory?

What drives someone to tape every episode of their favourite soap or comedy show on TV so they can watch them again and again or to spend night after night drinking and chatting in loud and smoky pubs and wine bars?

Are we alone in our fascination with how different people live their lives? We suspect not. Think of your family and friends, and the people in your local community. How many of them do the same things as you, share the same interests, and think as you do or have the same basic beliefs? We suspect the similarities grow fewer the further you look from your own social centre. Even within a family or group of close friends, while there is often much in common, the richness of difference is still there. How many of us have husbands, wives or partners whose view of the world we find difficult to understand, or have brothers or sisters whose lives lead them along paths we would not dream of following?

Consider all the people you know at work or the people you interact with on a daily basis. How many do you feel share a similar perspective to your own? Do the people doing the same job as you do it in the same way or look to get from it the same satisfactions? What about people in other teams or departments? What are they like, what attracts them to the work they do? Are there jobs within your company that you would not have at twice the salary, jobs that would drive you crazy within a week? Yet there are people doing those jobs and getting fulfilment from them. Are there other jobs you would prefer to do because they would fulfil you more than the one you hold at present?

This book is about people. It is about how we all strive to fulfil our needs, both in work and in our broader lives. It is about understanding something of the complexity of you and me so that we can make choices about how to get the rewards we want, whatever they are.

Hilltops

Rather than get involved in the intricacies of a variety of psychological theories, we have developed an image to convey in a simple yet profound way this whole notion of individuality and uniqueness. This image we have labelled 'Hilltops'.

The basic premise is that everyone on this planet stands on their own unique hilltop from which they peer out and view the world. Each one of us has, quite literally, a point of view that no-one else shares. There may be people who have hilltops that are quite close to each other and who can agree on many things (we will deal with this later) but there is no-one who shares the exact point from which you view the world. Even at a simple physical level, two people can't occupy exactly the same place at the same time, so when viewing the same object or event each must have a slightly different angle on it.

No-one can get inside your skin or look out through your eyes. If we add to this the well-accepted notion that perception is not simply a passive event – that we do not act like a camera faithfully capturing objective data but select, interpret and evaluate all that bombards us – then perhaps we are starting to get a glimpse of how unique our view of the world really is.

Exercise

Stop reading for a moment and look around. Where are you? Are you sitting, standing, lying down? Are you in a room, outdoors, or travelling somewhere? Describe the environment: what is it like?

Are there other people around? If so, who are they? What do you know of them? If you were to give a thumbnail sketch of them, what would you say?

By completing the above exercise you will have just produced something unique in the world. Not another living person would have described what you just have. Right now there is no-one else having the same experience as you. You might be reading this on a train or bus, crammed with people, all apparently having a similar experience, but they are not experiencing it from your hilltop, only from theirs. For example, some may be finding it a tense and overcrowded journey, others part of an exciting visit to a tourist site, while some might be virtually oblivious to it.

Where do hilltops come from?

If we accept the idea that we all have a unique hilltop, then it is worth understanding where it has come from. In short, how have I ended up being me?

We could, of course, devote this whole book to development theories, what different schools of psychology say about learning, and the growth of personality. There is, for example, the long-standing debate on genetic inheritance versus social conditioning – are we born with certain attributes or are they created by our environment? Our position is that, whatever the truth, we may never know or need to know. What is important is that we develop a detailed understanding of where we are now, of our own personal hilltops.

 Exercise

Ask yourself, 'How come I have ended up being here, doing this particular work at this particular point in my life? What chance happenings, acts of will, or seized opportunities have led me here?'

Now, the question in this exercise is a serious one and an autobiography could be written to answer it. Again, one thing is certain: the simple fact that no-one else in the world will describe what you would describe in your story; no-one in the world has lived your life. There is no-one in the world who sees things in quite the same way as you, not even your colleagues who are doing an identical job. No-one else looks through your eyes.

Values and beliefs

Over the years, as we grow from a little molehill to (in some cases) a veritable mountain, we develop a sense of what we like and dislike, what's good and bad, right and wrong, important or meaningless. What develops in the core of our hilltop is in fact a set of values and beliefs. These may change over time, but at any point in our lives we all have a core set of values and beliefs that are central to our hilltop.

For many of us, in the normal course of daily life, our central beliefs and values are rarely the subject of introspection – life is too fast for that. We choose, we decide, we make judgments and take action without conscious reference to them. However, they are always there, acting as an inner template for all of our activities. For example, 'I value my department or organisation, therefore I defend it when it is attacked,' or 'I value life, the lives of others and my car, therefore I always drive with care'.

We all have values and beliefs at the core of our hilltop. They govern all we do.

If you accept the idea that your hilltop is a product of the unique tapestry of your life, of all your experiences, knowledge, feelings, values, preferences and prejudices, then you will inevitably conclude that your hilltop governs two all-embracing activities – what you perceive and what you express – or, more simply, what you take in and what you give out.

The filters of the mind

Whatever your hilltop is, it will affect the way you see things. If you value justice you will look for fairness in your transactions. If you value winning you will look for opportunities to compete. If you value rationality you will look for the logic in arguments.

When people take on a role, they add to their hilltop a role perception. This makes them see things from a different angle. So, a marketing expert does not watch an advertisement from the same perspective as the consumer it is aimed at. An accountant sees a financial report differently from a salesperson. A production line operator sees his or her company from a very different perspective to that of a managing director. *What we perceive is dictated by who we are.*

How many times have you been in meetings with people from different departments or different companies who interpret the same data in completely opposite ways? How many times do we witness the leaders of our political parties reaching totally different conclusions from the same basic 'facts'?

Have you ever had the experience of moving roles and changing your perspective on certain issues? Some people might have accused you of selling out, when in fact it was simply that the move allowed a different light to be cast on the issue.

It is amusing to see how many drivers completely change their perspective when they become pedestrians in busy town traffic. As drivers, we have got enough to watch out for in traffic, without reckless pedestrians throwing themselves onto the road. However, as pedestrians we complain bitterly when drivers show no consideration for us waiting to cross, and are prepared to march on to pedestrian crossings with an undying faith in the rule of the right of way.

Do you know people who have a particular brand of 'ism' – environmentalism, sexism, racism, capitalism, chauvinism etc? Whatever the focus, an 'ism' is an encapsulation of a belief system, core values in a person's hilltop. This produces a certain perspective when the person is confronted by any data, a television programme, newspaper article, incident, etc. All are subjected to the same process of evaluation, interpretation and reaction based on that particular hilltop. What an 'ism' does basically is govern how things are understood, what *meaning* is taken from the data. The stronger the 'ism', the more it limits any other possible interpretation being considered.

You may, of course, think that 'isms' are too extreme to be used as examples to illustrate the hilltop concept, and you may be right. There are many people who, justifiably, would claim not to have such strong beliefs.

So, how do you personally make judgments about things? How, for example, do you form opinions about what your company or department is doing? What is the basis on which you judge a thing to be right or wrong? On what basis do you make decisions?

 ## Exercise

Take any issue about which you have an opinion (it can be domestic, work, political, social – it doesn't matter what the focus is).

Instead of describing or explaining your opinion, ask yourself why you think or feel that way about the issue. Ask yourself what belief system underpins your position. Ask why again and again, until you can say 'Because I believe that.'

Finding what we want to find

Another interesting phenomenon we have observed is the idea that what we see is in no small measure dictated by what we look for. Have you ever had the experience of buying something, such as a model of car or mobile phone, that you had never noticed before, and found that suddenly you see it everywhere? The simple fact of owning one suddenly makes them highly visible! Of course they were there all the time but only attracted your attention when they became in some way relevant to you, a little piece of your identity.

What about the way we view other people? What lies at the basis of how you form opinions of others? When you think of the people you admire, what is it that you admire about them? And what is it that you find distasteful about the people you do not like?

Exercise

I admire people who are:

....

....

....

....

....

....

....

....

....

....

I do not admire people who are:

....

....

....

....

....

....

....

....

....

....

What does this exercise tell you about your own value system?

It is interesting that no matter who you have as your heroes, they will probably be someone else's villains. What you see in people that you value is seen very differently by others and perhaps devalued. The same qualities are being described from different hilltops: confident becomes arrogant, determined becomes ruthless, persuasive becomes manipulative, self-assured becomes egotistical, warm becomes phoney, studious becomes pedantic, sensitive becomes sentimental, dynamic becomes macho, committed becomes tunnel-visioned, freedom-fighting becomes terroristic.

The point is that how we judge others is not based on external 'facts' that everyone agrees on, but on the things that each of us looks for and values in other people. How we judge others is more dependent on our own hilltop than on their behaviour. We know a businessman who actually seems to trust no-one in the world, except perhaps his wife and dog (and we are not even sure about that). From his hilltop, therefore, when he peers out of his office window at his customers, staff and sales people, he finds his world full of untrustworthy people.

Now, you may have a hilltop that resists the notion that we judge others, feeling that it is in some way wrong to judge. However, it can be possible to judge others without the negative connotations usually associated with the word 'judgment'. Similarly, the word 'discrimination' has in our society taken on an ugly meaning, while the true usage of these words denotes some of the higher powers of the human mind: without the ability to make judgments or to discriminate between things we simply could not learn.

If you find yourself in a recruitment situation, or a position in which you have to choose between people, what do you look for above and beyond the job specification? We all know the tendency, particularly in long-established organisations, to recruit in one's own image and in new entrepreneurial organisations to recruit in the image of the founder members. There are thousands of people who never get promoted because they do not match the template their immediate superior has of someone 'fitted' or 'suited' to a higher post. There are many organisations where the recruitment focus asks, 'Are they our kind of person?'

So in summary, having a hilltop, whatever it may be, governs our perception of the world. It determines how we see things, how we view others or interpret events. It determines what we look out for and what we consider to be important.

We realise that this may sound obvious and, in some ways, pure common sense. However, we have found that such sense is not that common. We actually meet few people who clearly demonstrate that they are aware that what they experience is *only* what they experience, and not necessarily the definitive version. How often do you hear people say things like: 'No, you're wrong', or 'In actual fact, the truth of the matter is' rather than, 'My perception of it is like this…' or 'What I experienced was….'

Broadcasting your hilltop

Our hilltop determines how we perceive things. The second all-embracing activity that hilltops govern is what we give out, what we broadcast.

We are all brilliant broadcasters. Broadcasting is something we do all the time, something that we cannot help doing. Even the strong silent types among us are constantly broadcasting they are strong silent types!

Everything we do – the jobs we have, the cars we drive, the companies we work for – all tell their story. The friends we have, the partners we are attracted to, where we live – all are broadcasting something about who we are.

 Exercise

Think about the clothes you wear to work. Ask yourself 'What do they broadcast about me?' (If you're not sure of the answer, ask around!)

Think of the car you drive or, what is perhaps more revealing, the car you would *like* to drive. What is it that attracts you to it? Why are those attractive elements important to you? What statement is that making about your hilltop?

As we have already demonstrated, how these broadcasts will be received by someone else is another matter, and something we will address when we discuss the difficulties of communicating successfully across the chasm between different world views. Someone sitting quietly in a group discussion, perhaps out of shyness or a lack of confidence, can very easily be perceived as aloof or disinterested. Others who feel keen and enthusiastic can appear dominating or insensitive – it all depends on who is doing the receiving.

If you have experienced any kind of interview you will know the litany of things to consider with regard to dress, manner, eye contact etc., and how important those things are in making an impression. There is a considerable amount of research which suggests that decisions are made in interviews within the first couple of minutes, the rest of the time being spent gathering data to confirm the initial judgment.

While many of us acknowledge this phenomenon, we tend to treat interviews as special events, i.e. times when we need to make a good impression. The truth is that we make impressions all the time, on everyone we contact. It's just the circumstance that makes them seem special.

This is particularly true in the case of giving opinions about things. Opinions are very revealing because they are direct expressions of our hilltop, our point of view. To plagiarise Newton, for every opinion there is an equal and opposite opinion, and you only have to watch a television debate to see the truth of this statement: the more contentious the topic, the more polarised the hilltops are.

Blind Men and the Elephant Story

It was six men of Hindustan
To learning much inclined,
Who went to see the Elephant
(Though all of them were blind),
That each by observation
Might satisfy his mind.

The first approached the Elephant
And happening to fall
Against his broad and sturdy side,
At once began to bawl,
'Bless me it seems the Elephant
Is very like a wall!'

The second feeling of his tusk,
Cried 'Ho, what have we here?
So very round and smooth and sharp?
To me 'tis mighty clear
This wonder of an Elephant
Is very like a spear.'

The third approached the animal
And happening to take
The squirming trunk within his hands,
Thus boldly up and spake;
'I see' quoth he, 'the Elephant
Is very like a snake!'

The fourth stretched out his eager hand
And felt about the knee:
'What most this mighty beast is like,
'Tis mighty plain' quoth he,
'Tis clear enough the Elephant
Is very like a tree.'

The fifth who chanced to touch the ear,
Said: 'Even the blindest man
Can tell what this resembles most;
Deny the fact who can,
This marvel of an Elephant
Is very like a fan!'

The sixth, no sooner had begun
About the beast to grope,
Than, seizing on the swinging tail
That fell within his scope,
'I see' quoth he, 'the Elephant
Is very like a rope.'

And so these men of Hindustan
Disputed loud and long,
Each in his own opinion
Exceeding stiff and strong.
Though each was partly in the right
And all were in the wrong!

J.G. Saxe (1816 – 1887)

The notion of rightness

The question we are left with is 'So who's right?' It is our experience that most people believe that if others saw things in the same way as they do, the world would be a far happier place! Are they in a minority, or do you think that too?

We have yet to meet anyone who believes that the way they see the world is wrong. We all believe our experience of the world to be true – we have to, it is the only experience we have.

Of course, there are people who would challenge the notion that 'I am right and the rest are wrong to some degree', and accept that the views of others are not wrong, simply different but equally valid. As discussions develop, such challengers often insist that their liberal tolerance of different yet equally valid perspectives is right! A hilltop that is prepared to accept other perspectives as equal and not to claim it has cornered the market on truth is, they claim, the *right* hilltop to stand on!

Hilltops and self-preservation

What happens when you challenge someone's hilltop position?

They start defending it. Battlements are rapidly built around the hilltop to protect its summit from assault. If the attack, or perceived attack, continues, the odd grenade may be tossed over the parapets. We do not grow our hilltop carefully over the years in order for it to be washed away by a sudden deluge, or flattened by someone else.

It is in the nature of a hilltop to confirm its rightness and to prevent change. If you doubt this idea, think of conflicts you have witnessed. People do not like being proved wrong, and, depending on what is at stake, will fight tooth and nail to defend their position.

Having said that, hilltops can – and do – change. They can change as part of a maturation process, or over time. They can grow as new experiences, awareness and understanding develop. They change as social attitudes change (or is it the other way round?). For example, there are many people today who have as part of their hilltop a 'green' awareness that was not there a decade ago. People no longer find it strange to sort their rubbish for recycling, to bring containers to the grocer to be filled, and thus to reduce packaging waste.

Basically, people change either through awareness or through pain. If a person has fixated on a particular hilltop, it may take some traumatic event to unlock the doors and allow the possibility of change, for it is difficult for most people to give up something that they have spent their lives developing. Habit, custom, tradition and history all offer a measure of comfort.

Change through awareness is a safer, though not necessarily easier, route because change demands some understanding of who you are, where you want to be, and how to get there.

The major focus for this book is on raising your awareness of who you are, what your hilltop is and how it shapes your life and, importantly, your approach to the work you do. It will enable you to assess your predominant drives, strengths and limitations, and allow you to make greater choices in the control of your career. It will allow you to start understanding something of what makes other people tick, so that you can gather sufficient insight into their hilltops to aid you in your dealings with them.

Summary

- We all stand on a unique hilltop from which we view the world.
- Our hilltop is built from our life experience.
- It has at its core our values and beliefs: they determine what we like and dislike, value or reject, judge as right and wrong.
- Our hilltop determines how we interpret information and events.
- Our hilltop determines how and what we broadcast to the world.
- We all believe that the way we see things is true.
- A function of a hilltop is to resist unwanted change.
- Hilltops can and do change through growth, maturation, awareness or pain.

CHAPTER 2

What Drives You? Basic 7P Types

So, people are unique. Like fingerprints, each person leaves his or her own unique expression in the world. We can all drink a toast to individuality.

However, this leaves us with lots of problems, the first being how do we make sense of people? If a person is unique, then how do we compare him or her with others, how do we judge what they do? How are we able to say what are strengths and what are weaknesses if everyone is a 'law unto themselves'? When we need to persuade someone to adopt a certain course of action, how can we do it successfully without first knowing all there is to know about that person's hill-top?

In the business environment there are many widely-used approaches to tackling this problem: psychometric tests, personality inventories, skill appraisal instruments, etc. All seek to identify key elements within the individual. However, the difficulty we have found is that most work situations do not afford the opportunity for such tests. It would, for example, be somewhat over-ambitious to expect an important customer to sit down to take a test so that we could then know how we might best influence him or her.

The model which forms the basis of this book was developed to meet the needs of the here-and-now, 'live' business context; to give people within organisations a way of gleaning enough about another person to be able to understand something about their hilltop which will be *useful* in interactions with them. If you are in a position of managing staff, making group decisions with colleagues, persuading and influencing others, or simply getting on with people, it is very helpful to know something about who you are dealing with.

We all know that it is possible to say the same thing in lots of different ways. Some ways will work with some people and not with others; some ways will get right up someone's nose! It all depends on who you are talking to, what you say and how you say it. Think of the people you know best: do you know how to say things for best effect, or definitely how not to say something if you don't want a fight on your hands? The message is simple: the more we know about someone, the better the chance of predicting how they will respond.

In most situations it is impossible to know our colleagues as well as we know our nearest and dearest. We simply do not have the time, or perhaps the inclination, for such relationships. The question, then, is what do we need to know about them to enable us to be more effective in our dealings with them? The answer, we believe, lies in understanding something of the core of a person's hilltop, their drives, motivations and values. These are the elements that determine how a person perceives their world and the positions they adopt.

A manager, for instance, might be discussing a restructuring of workloads with three team members. The first might have a hilltop that values order and clarity. She will press for detailed procedures and job descriptions. The second one's hilltop values team spirit and co-operation. He is therefore concerned that work is allocated fairly and amicably. The third has a hilltop that values personal success and achievement. Thus she is looking for a role that challenges her.

As in the Blind Men and the Elephant story, three different perspectives will be brought to bear on the same situation, each being concerned from a very different angle, each viewing the issue in a very different way. To effectively handle such a meeting the manager needs to know what is important to each individual, what the concerns are likely to be and how he or she might respond appropriately to each.

Such information, however, is not usually the first thing that is readily declared. While we do meet people who literally seem to wear their values on their sleeves, for most they are not the first things to be displayed. As already mentioned, for a lot of the time our values and drives simply are not the subject of our conscious attention. Another phenomenon we have observed is that people are not trained to pay conscious attention to looking for them. How often do you consciously stop listening to what someone is saying to appreciate who the person is that is saying it? We tend to listen to the broadcast and not the broadcaster. It is possible to retune our attention to a different frequency, to pay attention to a different quality of information that is being given out. People broadcast all the time – the secret is in being able to hear the broadcaster behind the messages.

In general, we are very perceptive animals. We pick up a lot of unspoken messages, body language, intuitive feelings that go on all the time below the surface messages. By making the broadcaster the subject of our conscious attention we can very quickly learn to spot the clues and signals that portray a person's hilltop. By looking at what people do and the way they do it, and by understanding what they get out of doing it, we can gain valuable clues about what drives them – which in turn tells us what needs consideration in our dealings with them.

And of course, the same holds true for us. If we are prepared to look at our behaviour and what lies behind it, we can understand why we do what we do, what's important, and what needs consideration in our dealings with ourselves.

Motivation or drive?

The path we take in understanding ourselves and others is through understanding the motivations and drives that are central to our behaviour. We do not intend to spend time in this book discussing the merits of the various motivation theories that have been espoused over the years, or even to get into deep debate about the fine distinctions that have been made between motivation and drive. We will use motivation and drive interchangeably to describe those factors within our hilltop that 'energise behaviour and give it direction'. In short, they are those urges that make us go after what we want or need in our lives.

Whether we call them drives or motives, they are fundamental forces that shape our approach to life and therefore our efforts to achieve what we feel to be important.

 Exercise

Think about what is important for you in your life. What do you value? Can you make a list of the things you value?

Drives – such as wanting to be recognised and valued, to be secure or to belong, or to explore and experience – are very different. They motivate individuals who hold very different values, and therefore have different perspectives on life. In relationships and in our careers, our drives dictate what we are attracted to and what we avoid, the manner in which we operate, and how we interact with other people whose drives are different.

The 7Ps of drive

According to all of the major research, there are actually very few fundamental drives. If this is true (and *our* research over the years supports it), then exploring and understanding what our drives are is a powerful way of discovering some core elements of our hilltop. We have found that the basic drives can be usefully categorised into seven discreet groups which we label as **Product**, **People**, **Process**, **Power**, **Plans**, **Positioning**, and **Purpose**.

We are aware of the problem of definition in any kind of labelling. Having just read these labels, possibly for the first time, what do they mean from your hilltop? Some of them may seem obvious, others may be meaningless. We have contemplated many ways of labelling these drives: numbering, lettering, colouring, characters like 'Inscrutable Protagonist', etc. All have their drawbacks.

The major reason for choosing the 7Ps is that we use this model when consulting with client companies across a wide spectrum of organisational activities, looking at how drive manifests itself at different levels – from the individual, to the team, to departments, to divisions, or to the organisation as a whole. They are labels on the map to give us a common language with which to describe the reality of the terrain. The next chapters will attempt to enliven each of these labels by painting the extraordinary richness of the ways in which these drives manifest themselves.

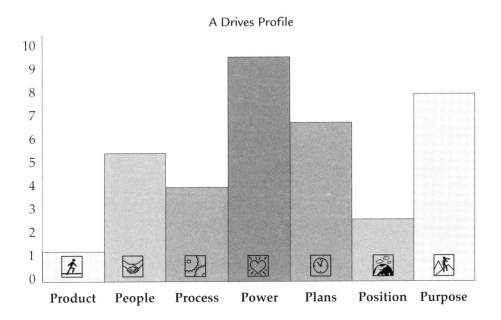

A Drives Profile

A drives profile

The theories of motivation most widely used in business are still based around the paradigm that is embraced by Abraham Maslow's *Hierarchy of Needs.* If you are familiar with his work you will find direct parallels between some of his drive states and the 7Ps. However, rather than describe these drives as hierarchical, with all the possible connotations, we prefer to use the notion of a profile to convey the relationship they have to everyday behaviour.

This is not to suggest we disagree with Maslow's premise that the 'lower' drives need to be satisfied before 'higher' drives can be engaged. It is simply that we do not wish to present these different drives as being higher or lower, better or worse than each other.

The dynamics of drive

Thinking of these drives in a bar graph or profile form introduces the idea of them being in a *dynamic* rather than a *static* state. It is clear that during any day or week some drives are stronger at times than others. For example, after sitting doing paperwork all day the drive for some form of physical activity could be greater than usual; after a week of organisational chaos, the need for a bit of peace and quiet might be paramount. Our drives are not simple constants, they ebb and flow in strength depending on how well they are satisfied by our daily activities.

What it takes to satisfy any particular drive in an individual also varies enormously, depending on the strength of the drive. Drives can be small or massive, and some people never satisfy them. There are some people who can never seem to get enough of a particular thing, whose drive in a certain area seems immense. There are people within the Information Technology industry, for example, who describe computing as an addiction. Yet there are other people who cannot read a newspaper article about the subject without experiencing acute boredom. Similarly, there are people we meet who never seem to be still, who are driven to constant activity and who become frustrated and irritated if they cannot be up and doing. And there are people with very low 'doing' drives: 'Let me sit and ponder, consider and plan'.

Competing drives

Because we are complex creatures, our drives often compete with each other and cause that awful situation in decision making known as the 'dither point'.

We meet many middle managers who suffer from drive competition. On the one hand they have a drive to do a sound job, be task-oriented and achieve results; on the other they have a need to be people-centred, to be liked and accepted by their staff. Marrying the two is often quite difficult. This leads to the idea (which we will explore in Chapter 14) that in many ways these different drives are mutually exclusive and that when drives are competing, either within you or between you and someone else, the outcome is often conflict.

Satisfaction of drives

As we have already said, our drives are some of the core elements within our hilltop. What we are starting to describe using the drive profile is some of the complexity within each of us that gives rise to our behaviour. We are driven in our behaviour – both long and short term – by the intricate make-up of our profile. The range of activities, interests and behaviours that the human race engages in during the pursuit of satisfying these drives is truly impressive. And of course, not all behaviour in the world is what we would consider positive. There is a continuum of behaviours for each of the drives which we would describe as positive and negative. We are aware of the possibility of this being perceived as a value judgment – we too have our hilltops. However, to define positive and negative a little more, we might say that something is *positive* when it is:

- Inclusive rather than exclusive
- Constructive rather than destructive
- Confirmatory rather than critical
- Empowering rather than impoverishing
- Expansive rather than diminishing

The notion of types

Do you believe there are different types of people? Developing typologies can be a fraught business: whenever a membrane is drawn around a set of characteristics and called a *type*, there immediately arises the problem of *stereotyping*. Stereotyping is criticised for being unfair, limiting, a gross generalisation and usually extremely pejorative – which is often true. Nevertheless, in everyday life most of us seem to carry around some internal typology which we use to help us understand people.

We have typologies for everything stored in our memories, built up from years of experience: types of plants, animals, houses, problems, etc. Developing types is an integral part of the learning process, often referred to as 'pattern recognition'. Without the ability to recognise patterns in things, learning can only take place by trial and error. Without pattern recognition, without being able to group characteristics together or discriminate between them, all snakes are poisonous and all mushrooms edible! Obviously, trial and error can be a very costly affair.

Inevitably, then, we develop some framework for types of people. The issue is how we improve the *quality* and *relevance* of a typology map to serve ourselves and others more effectively. Developing typologies need not imply limitation, generalisation and constraint. Putting a 'type' label on a person, object or event is only a problem if you do it with minimal data – so that all of the English are passionate about cricket, all BMW drivers aggressive, etc. This is a patently ludicrous pastime, indulged in by people who are not prepared to learn about others or themselves.

To classify people *only* by where they live, their occupation, or social status, etc. is to deny a wealth of difference between individuals – but that does not mean that such data has nothing at all to say. As we have already said, everything we do broadcasts something about who we are. The key is in understanding the individual motives behind behaviour, i.e. what someone gets out of doing what they do, living where they live, etc. Being able to spot the drives behind the behaviour is, in our experience, a more accurate way of describing a type.

Types and predominance

We have introduced the idea of a drive profile with which to plot your own individual drives, and the rest of the book will enable you to do just that. We have also suggested that the profile changes as drives increase or decrease. However, what has become apparent to us in using this approach is that most people we work with appear to have only one, two or three of these drives that predominate in their lives. It is as though we each live in a seven-roomed house but choose to spend most of our time just in a couple of them. Living in certain rooms produces a profile with those drives as the predominant features of our make-up.

If a typology is possible in drive analysis then it stems from this idea of predominance. This does not imply that people are limited to the rooms they live in – they potentially have access to them all – but living in certain rooms, seeking to fulfil certain drives, gives rise to predictable qualities and characteristics in their ways of behaving.

It also gives rise to the idea of self-limitation. For whatever reason, most of us have some rooms that we find it difficult to enter, or feel uncomfortable in, or – in extreme cases – the door to which seems locked and we have lost the key. For example, there are people who find social situations very awkward, who do not have access to the drive that is concerned with belonging that is nourished by social contact. To such people, the office party can be an ordeal. There are others who actively avoid acclaim and recognition for outstanding achievements. There are others with very little physical drive, for whom activity or work of a physical nature is gross and demeaning.

Spotting drives

If we continue for a moment with the house analogy, it is often easy to spot the predominant drives that people display because it is possible to see which rooms they are living in – they are the ones with the lights on. What is broadcast from the different rooms can be seen clearly with the trained eye.

A word of extreme caution, however: what a person *does* may not supply enough data to enable judgments to be made about their predominant drives. For example, the fact that a person goes out every Sunday with his family does not tell you everything about his drives. Not even *how* a person does it can tell you for sure. The key, as already mentioned, is *why* he does it – in short, what he gets out of that behaviour.

The same applies to you. It would be easy to skim the following chapters and, on superficial data, decide what your own drives are, what 'type' of person you are. Yet the most difficult people to assess clearly are yourself and the people you know best, because of the vast amount of exposure you have to yourself and those close to you: you see many different facets, a multi-dimensional being. With someone new, it is often much easier to see which drives are shining the brightest.

Self-development

This book is about taking stock, empowerment and choice. By developing a thorough understanding of your personal drive profile, you can actively choose to:

A) Change your situation to nourish the drives you have
B) Develop and nurture some of your more recessive drives
C) Be content with who and where you are

Whatever your choice, if this book is to be of real value, then we encourage you to spend some time involving yourself in a worthwhile exploration. You will certainly end up knowing more about why you do what you do, even if you choose the option C above. Furthermore, you will gain great insight into the people around you so that if you choose A, you will already have a head start on developing ways of communicating with them more effectively. If you choose option B then you will benefit from the clear guidance on the kinds of activities you can engage in to develop yourself.

Summary

- The more we know about ourselves and others, the better the chance of being able to predict responses.
- Understanding drives is the key to understanding people; they are fundamental aspects of our hilltop.
- We can identify seven basic drives: Product, People, Process, Power, Plans, Positioning and Purpose.
- We all have the seven drives within us.
- Drives are in a dynamic state of balance.
- Drives can range in strength from virtually non-existent to immense.
- Drives often compete with each other, causing decision-making difficulties.
- People set about trying to satisfy their drives through an infinite variety of behaviours.
- Observing behaviour alone is not enough to understand individual drives.
- A typology emerges from a person's predominant drives.
- The drives that are the strongest dictate more of the behaviour of the individual as he or she seeks to fulfil his or her needs.

CHAPTER 3

The Three-Level Technique, Listening and Questioning

In the last chapter we introduced the idea that types can be understood by looking at which drives predominate in the make-up of a person's unique drive profile. We also described the dangers inherent in labelling people as certain types with very little data on which to base those judgments. If we are to make use of the idea that people are unique, yet have similarities, we need to be able to gather enough quality information with which to make accurate distinctions. If we really want to know what drives behaviour, what causes people to hold a particular outlook on life, we need to look for the right kinds of information. This is equally important whether we are trying to understand other people or ourselves.

*What people **do** cannot tell you enough. Not even **how** they do it. What is really important is **why** they do it.* If you truly want to understand anyone, yourself included, you need to go beyond observable behaviour to understand the *meaning* of that behaviour – what motivates them to do what they do?

For many years, when working with groups in training situations, we have taught a powerful yet simple technique for gathering such quality information. Originally we taught it as a diagnostic technique to be used by consultants, managers, recruitment and appraisal specialists – in short, by anyone whose job entailed them understanding, or getting things done through others. For obvious reasons, it became known as the Three-Level Technique or 3LT for short. Our programmes were consistently rated by the participants as very valuable and meaningful to their work. However, what began to intrigue us was this regularly-voiced comment: 'I've learned a lot about myself this week'.

When we began checking why that was so, we realised that in introducing the idea of hilltops and the 3LT, people were starting to use it to reflect on their own behaviour and motives. It had touched them by raising awareness of themselves. What started out as a technique for gathering information about others had become a very powerful way of allowing people to reflect on themselves.

We are introducing it into this book as a discovery tool, a tool which you can use to reflect on your own drives and to understand the drives of others.

Throughout the following chapters we have included a range of questions aimed at raising awareness of your own drive states. They cannot hope to cover every circumstance of each individual reader. If, however, you grasp 3LT and use it, you will find it can be applied across the spectrum of your behaviour – from the largest life decision to the smallest detail. If you become skilful in its use when dealing with other people, it will enable you to spot predominant drives and hill-top positions very accurately, and prevent you from making gross assumptions about why people do what they do.

The Three-Level Technique (3LT)

The most effective way of learning this technique is to do it. This first exercise will take five minutes, and you will need a pen and paper.

 Exercise

Choose something that you have an interest in. (It might be a hobby, a work activity, or anything, but it must be something that you actively engage in.)

Level 1   Write down some of the facts about your involvement in this interest, e.g. what you do, where, when, how often, who with, etc.

Level 2   Look at the facts of what you do and now ask, 'What do I get out of doing this?' (You will probably generate several things – make a list.)

Level 3   Look at your answers to Level 2. If you have a list, choose one which you feel is the most important. Now ask yourself this question about that Level 2 item: 'Why is that important to me as a person?'

In doing this exercise you may have found the Level 1 answers easy to generate, while Levels 2 and 3 became progressively harder. You may have found yourself contemplating those questions for the first time. If you look at your second and third level answers it is clear that they are not about the activity but about you as a person, about your motives around that particular interest. If you want to, you can go back to your Level 2 list and take all the other items through the same process.

Many other people who share the same interest might give similar Level 1 answers to yours. Developing a typology on the basis of Level 1 facts – observable behaviour – could lead us to assume that all people who pursue that interest are the same, which is patently untrue. If we are to differentiate more accurately, it is the deeper quality of information we must understand. This simple technique identifies the drives that the interest satisfies and the values behind them, i.e. what is important to us as individuals. Using this process allows us to spot differences and recognise why each of us does the things we do.

Below is an example of using 3LT to understand an individual's specific interest in squash.

 Example: Squash

Level 1   What is your involvement in squash?
'Member of my local squash club. Play in league competitions, fourth division out of seven in the club. I play twice a week, one league match, another usually against one of a handful of regular opponents. Played for six years, and have got to a stage where I am contemplating having some professional coaching to improve my game.'

Level 2   What do you get out of doing it?
'Keeping fit, it's a good workout
A chance to let off steam
Competition
Social contact
Improving my skill
Occasional business contacts'

Which is the most important?
'Improving my skill is the main enjoyment. I obviously like to win, but I would rather play well and lose than win but play badly. I would rather play people who stretch me than beat someone easily.'

Level 3   Why is improving your skill important to you?
'Because I like to stretch myself. I think it is important to strive to be as good as I can be in whatever I do.'

The 3LT is based on the premise that when people describe things, they give out different qualities of information. We have found it useful to distinguish three distinct levels of information: Facts, Meaning and Importance.

Level 1 – Facts

In most situations, external, factual information provides the major part of our communication. What happened, what is in the report, where I have been today, the latest news etc. When people talk, they invariably tell you the what's, when's and where's about the subject, even if it is themselves. Dealing with facts, passing on raw data, is a fundamental part of communication. However, if we need to understand *who* is doing the talking, we need better quality information.

Level 2 – Meaning

Information at this level crosses the boundary between external facts and internal feelings. Level 2 information is about the meaning, interest or feelings about those facts to the individual concerned. It starts to tell you something about the person who is describing the facts.

Level 3 – Importance

When you receive this information, you are getting a clear statement of one aspect of the person's hilltop position: what is important to that individual, why they value certain things, what they believe, etc. For example, 'it's very important that I…' or 'I believe that we all should….'

Using 3LT

We have described 3LT as a discovery tool. To develop a clear picture of your own hilltop you need to use it to reflect on your own behaviour; on your perspective, your opinions and attitudes: '*Why* do I do that, *why* do I feel that, *why* is that important to me?' and so forth.

Using 3LT demands a willingness to look at ourselves and our responses, a willingness that some people do not have. It also calls for a degree of honesty with ourselves when we find motives that we dislike: as we have already said, we can be our own worst judges. We judge some of our drives as good or bad, and ascribe to ourselves faults that others may consider attributes. In the following chapters we hope to cast a non-judgmental eye over the drives we see in people, to identify strengths and limitations rather than rights or wrongs.

The same is demanded when you use it to look at what other people do – willingness, honesty and the ability to suspend judgment. In fact, if you are unable to suspend judgment then you will find out little about yourself or anyone else: the reason for most people not declaring their deeper thoughts and feelings is the fear of being judged. If you ask people questions and then judge their responses, you will very quickly close the conversation down.

We are not saying that you must never make judgments, but that it is important to suspend making them for long enough to gather quality information. This will enable more informed and accurate judgments to be made at a later stage.

Listening

Good listeners are few and far between. Being a good listener means more than being able to repeat or even paraphrase what has been said. In our terms, good listeners are people who can pay attention to the *messenger,* not just the *message.* We cannot really listen to someone unless we are able to temporarily suspend judgment – a far more difficult task than it may appear. This means setting aside our own hilltop perspective, our own prejudices and values, so that we can, as far as possible, enter the other person's inner world to glimpse their reality rather than our own. Good listening is achieved by giving absolute attention to the speaker. Most of the time we do not do this. We fill our thoughts with our own agenda, waiting for a pause to give our response, or we filter the messages through our own belief systems and respond with questions aimed at changing the speaker's mind, saying for example, 'Yes, I understand that, but don't you think that....'

Good listeners are those who can look behind the words to the meaning and implications of what is being said. The 3LT is a powerful discovery tool: the very act of consciously attending to the search for meaning improves the quality of listening tremendously. It allows us to sort out what is being disclosed when a person is speaking and to spot the different qualities of information that are being given to us.

Listening is probably the most undervalued skill we can develop. The alternative to listening is to interrupt or to leap to assumptions based on selective hearing. When a person talks, he or she offers opportunities to understand them as individuals, not just the subject they are talking about. If you can retune your ears to listen for these different levels of information, people will describe themselves to you even in the most apparently mundane conversations.

Questioning

Of course, some people are much more voluble than others. Some wear their values on their sleeves and find it difficult to hold a conversation without publicly declaring what they believe. For others however, 3LT can be used to spot opportunities to ask deeper-level questions. We call these opportunities 'permission points' – usually small throw-away comments or little additions to the main body of Level 1 information, for example, '… and I found it quite interesting', or '…and I think it's important'.

What these permission points do is invite you to pick them up and ask a deeper question, for example, 'What was it about it that interested you?', or 'Why do you think it is important?'

Levels of questions

Just as we can use 3LT to sort and understand information that is being voluntarily given to us, so we can use it as a framework actively to gather information from these different levels.

- *Level 1 questions* are about facts, data, specific information, e.g. what, where, when, who, how often.
- *Level 2 questions* are about the meaning those facts have. They are questions to elicit feelings, likes and dislikes, preferences, views and opinions about the facts, e.g. 'What does that mean to you?' or 'What interests you about that?' or 'What do you feel about it?'
- *Level 3 questions* are aimed at understanding why the Level 2 answers are important to that individual. They elicit values, beliefs and attitudes, e.g. 'Why is that important to you?' or 'Why do you feel that?' or 'Why does that concern you?'.

Listening and questioning are skills that take practice. Most of the people we work with, while highly trained and competent in what they do, are rarely familiar with asking these kinds of questions. It takes effort to become skilful at questioning, and there are many different ways of phrasing the questions. If you take time to absorb this approach into your particular style it can become a natural part of your conversation.

We encourage you to apply 3LT throughout this book to deepen your inquiry around the topics that are raised. Before moving on to the drive chapters, it is worth doing a short 3LT exercise which you can then review after you finish reading the book.

 Exercise

What do you do?
(Describe the details of the work you do)

What do you get out of doing it?
(Describe the rewards, satisfactions, enjoyments and interests)

Why is that important to you as an individual?
(Describe why you value those rewards, satisfactions etc.)

Summary

- *Why* people do things – not *what they do* or *how they do it* – is what counts if you really want to understand them.
- The key is to dig beneath observable behaviour and get to its meaning, i.e. what motivates that behaviour.
- You can use the Three Level Technique (3LT) discovery tool to understand yourself as well as others.
- People give out three levels of information about their behaviour: *facts* ('out there', data), *meaning* ('in here', feelings) and *importance* (values, beliefs, attitudes).
- To get good quality information you must suspend judgment (leave your hilltop) while you collect it. Honesty and willingness to look at things without judging are important.
- The best listeners pay attention to both the messenger and the message. As they listen, they focus absolutely on these, rather than their own message or response. They analyse later.
- Questioning skills can actively deepen the quality of information you get from a person. Watch for 'permission points' and ask a deeper question.
- Both listening and questioning skills improve with practice.

PART 2

DRIVES, THE 7PS AND YOUR DRIVE PROFILE

CHAPTER 4

The 7Ps of Drive

We are now going to introduce seven archetypal hilltops: seven types created by the predominance of distinctly different drives. We ask you not to simply believe us, not to take a leap of faith and accept that these exist, but to *check it out for yourself.*

Listen to people you interact with. Listen for the deeper quality information they give you. Ask people questions; if they express enjoyment over something, ask them what it is that they enjoy. Watch the television with different eyes and ears, particularly biographical documentaries and interviews. Watch studio discussions and listen to the different hilltops being broadcast.

However, as we have said, perhaps the most difficult person to understand is yourself. Working to understand people other than yourself will attune you to the subtleties of your own different drives. As you explore the following chapters, you will find a series of self-awareness questions. These are designed to encourage you to reflect on how strongly the characteristics and qualities of each drive are reflected in the way you behave. They also focus on how much your work allows those drives to be satisfied.

You are about to enter what could be some quite alien worlds. There are people you pass every day in the street and people at work whose hilltops are absolutely foreign to you. These people may look similar to you, they may even do similar kinds of work. But their perspectives, values and drives may be something that you simply will not identify with.

In the following chapters we will attempt to portray the richness that lies within each of the seven drive states, and how this produces qualities and characteristics that are noticeably different from each other.

It is a difficult task: words are not the best vehicle for describing some of the drives. If we could give you direct experience of them, if we could take you into places in society where you never go, if we could wrest you from your own mindset to experience what it feels like in these different states, we would.

Depending on your individual hilltop, on how much you operate from these various drives within yourself, you will find some of these worlds familiar and understandable, or strange and sometimes quite unbelievable. As you explore each chapter, try to relate the qualities and characteristics of each type to your own, or people that you know.

Monitor your reactions to the descriptions. Some you will appreciate and identify with, others you may notice yourself disliking or dismissing: these are important clues for you in building a picture of your own drive states.

It is impossible to do justice to the variety of human behaviour. We will often use examples of the kind of work that attracts different types, the typical roles or careers they develop, and how they tend to operate, etc. However they are only examples, they are not definitive 'boxes'. The different drives find expression in so many ways that it is impossible to catalogue them completely.

The focus of the following chapters is from the inside out. What we are really trying to do is to paint pictures of what is important and meaningful for each drive state – the Levels 2 and 3 of each type – and then describe some typical kinds of behaviour that are manifestations of each. The purpose is not to paint a complete portrait (which, in any case, would be impossible) but to allow the *essence* of each type to shine through so that you can begin to see it in people around you and, most importantly, in the things that you do. Throughout, the purpose is for you to reflect on how you relate to the drive in question.

If you are to get the most from this book, you must make some commitment of time and energy to finding the answers to the questions posed in the exercises. We suggest that you keep a notebook to record your thoughts as they will be needed in later chapters. By the end of each chapter you will not only have an insight into each drive but should know clearly how much this drive directs your life.

It is through the work you are prepared to do in these chapters that you will build your own drive profile.

Developing self-awareness is not a science: we have yet to find an instrument that adequately reflects the depth and subtlety of human experience. Our approach is to encourage you, through a series of questions and the use of 3LT, to explore your own world view and the drives that you exhibit.

The qualities needed to understand who you are a willingness to look at yourself, openness to the feedback you get from people around you, honesty with yourself and vigilance. It is important to be constantly vigilant, reassessing your reactions and responses to events in your life.

It is vital that you do not use the 7Ps of drive as labels to pigeonhole yourself, but as a map for self-awareness. If the 7Ps of drive are the map, 3LT is the magnifying glass. With these, you will be able to explore the complexity of your own terrain, and will be in a better position to make choices about your future.

It is not necessary to read the following chapters in linear order – in fact, there may be benefits in specifically not doing so. Look through the key word descriptions below and choose where you would like to start.

Product Drive
Action, physical activity, pragmatism, common sense.

People Drive
Friendship, caring, a sense of belonging, acceptance, loyalty.

Process Drive
Change, new experience, variety, intellectual stimulation.

Power Drive
Energy, commitment, challenge, success, recognition.

Plans Drive
Order, structure, logic, rationality, organisation.

Positioning Drive
Intuition, meaning, sensitivity, integration, balance.

Purpose Drive
Vision, mission, imagination, creativity.

CHAPTER 5

The Product Drive

Key traits: *Action, physical activity, exertion, stamina, pragmatism, common sense, health and fitness, bodily appearance, sexual and athletic prowess.*

Quite simply, the Product drive is the drive to produce, and to produce something *physical*.

Maslow identified this as the drive to satisfy physiological needs – hunger, thirst, sex, etc. We see it as the drive for all physical experience, the drive that primarily identifies us with our physical bodies and the physical world.

Predominance of the Product Drive

Of course we all have some of this drive within us. The question is, therefore, *how much* need do you have at the physical level? How much do you feel the need to eat when hungry, to quench your thirst, to maintain your health, to satisfy your sexual urges, and engage in physical activity? How Product-driven are you?

As we work through the characteristics and idiosyncrasies of the Product drive, relate them to your personal drive state. We will be describing the ways in which the Product drive manifests itself in behaviour. When we refer to the Product type, we mean someone who acts like this drive is the strongest drive in his or her profile.

Work

There is an age-old debate that surfaces whenever we discuss people and the types of work they do. One side of the argument holds that the role creates the person. The other, and the one we feel more aligned with, is that people are drawn to a certain occupation, one that seems to hold the possibility of doing something they enjoy or are competent at. It is true, however, that many jobs only require of a person certain attributes or skills, and for many people their leisure interests offer them the opportunity to fulfil the needs that work does not satisfy.

For people who have the Product drive as one of their predominant motives, the work that anyone does who is not 'on the shop floor' is, quite simply, not real work. Work is seen as physical labour, getting your hands dirty, producing something at the end of the day that you can see. Managers and supervisors, accountants and planners don't really work.

To a Product type, work is sheer physical labour, lifting and carrying, machining and manufacture, digging holes, building things, using heavy plant and machinery to get the job done. Work is done with the body as the primary tool.

Product-driven roles

The typical role occupied by a Product-driven person, therefore, is often the manual worker or the labourer. That is not to say that Product types are limited to these jobs, or that all manual workers are Product types. As we have said, we need to know what they get from the job, what the drive actually is, in order to make the distinction.

There are Product types in many walks of life: mechanics, skilled tradesmen, lorry drivers. Lots of Product types are attracted into the army. A surprising number of chefs we meet have strong Product drives. There are lots of Product-driven types in the booming fitness and leisure industry, athletic people who have found a job in leisure management. Many people who work out of doors – gardeners, farmers, fishermen and oil-riggers – are Product types.

The attraction is to working with physical things, whatever form it takes.

One of the primary differences between management and shop floor in most engineering or heavy industry is not one of class or politics; it is the hilltop of the Product-driven versus other hilltops we have yet to consider. One of the major criteria for credibility that any manager can have in such a situation is having been on the tools, being 'time-served', being able to roll up the old shirt sleeves and dig in. In fact, many people in such industries who have come from the point of actual direct contact in the field often voice their regret of not being able to produce directly any more.

 Self-awareness questions

What do you actually produce?

Does your work have a physical component?

If it has, use 3LT to explore what the physical aspect fulfils and why that is important.

You may have noticed that the roles described above have been, and in many cases still are, considered to be predominantly male occupations. In one heavy engineering company we were involved in recently, nearly all the women in an

8,000-strong workforce were either in the canteen or in the office. There was only one woman in the company who was a project manager in charge of a Production process.

Historically such work has been seen as the preserve of men. Whilst attitudes have changed in society at large, Product-driven work is still one of the bastions of maleness.

Indeed, the whole area of the Product drive has been riddled more than any other drive with taboos for both sexes, but especially for women. Until comparatively recently, in many Western societies at least, women have been conditioned into regarding the physical aspects of life as somewhat unwomanly. Whether we talk about the woman who wants to be an engineer or a construction worker, or the woman who commits her life to athletics, many have been seen as somewhat macho.

Do you remember the fuss made some years ago over the supposedly 'butch' female Russian athletes, rather than the acceptance and admiration given their male counterparts? This conditioning, for both sexes, goes back thousands of years to when men were seen as the hunters and warriors and most Product work was 'men's work'.

The Product type

We have focused for a while on the typical jobs that lend themselves to fulfilling the Product drive. If you do not do any physical work, however, this does not necessarily mean that you do not have a lot of Product drive within you. All it means is that the job you do probably has little 'Production' involved. To understand how Product-driven you are, we need to look beyond the confines of your role. To get behind the generalisation of 'all Product types are labourers' and vice versa, we need to look at the drive more closely, and examine some of the attitudes, values and perceptions that are associated with this predominance.

As we have already said, the major focus of this drive is on the body and on doing things physically. Product types, whether involved in physical labour or not, like taking action.

Many managers in Production-oriented organisations have the Product drive as a major part of their hilltop even if they no longer do the actual labour themselves. *Their focus is on getting the job done, making sure things happen.* They tend to be the people in meetings who want to get down to the nuts and bolts of what needs to happen, how and by when. They can be wonderfully pragmatic, identifying practical problems immediately (and often the solutions to them) in elegant operational plans.

Self-awareness questions

In your work, how much need do you have to make things happen?

How practical is your focus?

How often do you insist on tangible outcomes?

Use 3LT to explore your answers.

When your hilltop is dominated by a Product perspective, the only reality is the physical one. Neat theories are all very well but the bottom line is 'Will it work?' And in many cases, where planning is done without including such perspectives, the answer is 'No, of course it won't!'

Product types can be regarded by some other types as a tremendous asset in the planning situation because of their focus on practical realities. They can also be seen as nuisances for always wanting to bring pragmatism into an otherwise elegant design. Wise managers usually take care to tap Product types' pragmatism, while alining that input with the overall goals they are trying to achieve in the group.

A dog, journeying through a forest on an important errand, came to a wide river. In the tree above was a wise old owl. 'How am I going to get across here?' the dog asked the owl. The owl looked down from the tree and said, 'It's easy, all you have to do is turn yourself into a frog and swim across'. 'But how can I possibly do that?' demanded the dog. 'Don't ask me,' said the owl, 'I'm only the ideas man!'

A major benefit for those companies which have introduced practices such as 'quality circles' into their organisations is that they have provided a channel of expression for the intelligence and knowledge of the workers who are nearest the Product end. These are the people who can see the everyday physical problems, the inefficiencies that occur when plans are translated into physical reality. We use the word 'intelligence' here purposely. We find the word tends to be used to describe only certain kinds of intelligence – intellectual capacity in particular. This leads us to a focus on academic achievement and intellectual prowess as the main measures of success. To us, intelligence is the ability to respond appropriately in a given situation. *Each drive, and therefore each type, has its own kind of intelligence.*

Self-awareness questions

How much do you enjoy solving practical problems?
How at ease do you feel with physical work?
Do you regard yourself as having a lot of common sense?
Use 3LT to explore your answers.

Product types may not be good at solving abstract problems or dealing with concepts and ideas but will possess a high degree of intelligence in practical problem solving. They often possess an extraordinary ability to sort things out, to know the best way of tackling a certain job. Common sense is the intelligence of the Product type.

Limitations

What Product types are not good at is the more conceptual work involved with planning and processes. They can organise physical things or situations but tend not to be good at dealing with abstractions. They tend to get easily frustrated by lengthy discussions or endless meetings: talking rather than doing is seen as a waste of time. Product types have a strong dislike of apparent inactivity. If you work or live with a strongly Product-driven person, notice how twitchy or irritable they become if they cannot get on and 'do' something. Sitting down behind a desk can be torture for someone like this.

A limitation of people who predominate on Product and who do not have access to other drives is that many of them are not self-starters. They limit their activity to the physical aspect of organisations and often seem to say, 'Tell me what to do and let me get on with it. Making decisions and initiating ideas isn't my job.' With this attitude, they may either get really physically engaged and get on with the job, or may adopt an attitude to work which lacks any longer-term motive beyond the wage packet.

 Self-awareness questions

How often do you avoid physical work?
Do you get frustrated by lengthy discussion?
What motivates you to do physical work?
Use 3LT to explore your answers.

Leisure interests

As we said earlier, many jobs only require of a person certain attributes or skills, and many people use leisure interests to satisfy the drives that cannot be satisfied in their working environment. If we are going to understand the full range of drives that you exhibit, then we must explore the person outside of work, which may involve dealing with a whole different set of drives. This is particularly true of the Product drive; with so many jobs these days being in the service sector there are many Product types who find rewards through pursuits outside work.

One huge area of life that attracts people as an outlet for their Product drive is sport and physical pursuits. You will find people with a strong Product drive scattered widely across the sports fields and gymnasia of the world, fulfilling the need to be physically stimulated. How many people do you personally have contact with who take an active part in sport?

We are not saying that sport only serves to fulfil this particular drive – there are many satisfactions to be gained from many sports – but it is the physical aspect for the Product driven type that we want to focus on. Product types like physical exertion, they enjoy that feeling of pushing their bodies to the limit. The feeling of well-being that follows a hard physical workout is a wonderful sensation to Product-driven types. You will hear them saying things like 'I'm completely exhausted! That was great!'

 Self-awareness questions

How often do you feel the need to engage in physical activity?
How often do you actually do it?

Of course, not all sports attract such types. The distinction is in the degree of physical activity involved. Contact sports are the major magnets to Product types. Rugby (particularly rugby league), boxing, football, wrestling, American football – all have great appeal for Product types. Individual sports with high physical content – weight lifting, rock climbing, athletics, karate, etc. – also attract them. Sports which do not appeal are those with a comparatively low physical component, e.g. snooker, ice-skating, golf, bowls, etc.

We do not wish to give the impression that all Product types are madly keen sports people and under 30 years old. This is not the case (though age obviously affects the amount of physical activity people engage in). There are many

Product-driven types in the category of 'used to be' when it comes to active participation. So the question is, how else apart from sporting activity does the Product-driven type seek satisfaction of that drive?

 Self-awareness questions

Do you take part in any sports? Make a list of all the physical activities you engage in, both in and out of work.

Rank them in order of the most strenuous and physically demanding. Say how often you engage in them.

Ask yourself these 3LT questions about each one: 'What do I get out of doing them?' 'Why are the things I get from doing them important?'

Fitness and health

For many of us, including those whose Product drive is not the predominant one in our profile but is still very high, general good health and a degree of fitness is important. There has been a huge upturn over the last decade in the range of activities that are seen as accessible to all. The jogging phenomenon is a good example of how health-consciousness has increased in our society. The number of fitness studios, gym clubs and aerobics classes is another, and hotels that are primarily involved in the Business Conference market are falling over themselves to build leisure facilities into their amenities to cater for this growing trend.

Of course there are people who, for many reasons, would not visit such fitness facilities but prefer to gain Product fulfilment in other ways. For some this could be digging the garden, for others home decorating or remodelling. The satisfaction is not from physical exhaustion, but from having produced something tangible, something that you can see. Some people simply go for walks. Again, we need to stress that it is not simply the activity that dictates what drives the person doing it, it is the *motive* for doing it that is important. People go for walks for many more reasons than purely physical exercise.

 Self-awareness questions

How do you look after your health?

Do you do anything to keep fit?

Is good health and fitness important to you? If so, why?

Security

In Chapter 2 you were asked to make a list of the things that are important to you. Was there any evidence there of a Product drive? If you ask what is really important to a Product type, the bottom line is identification with themselves as a physical entity.

We all have some degree of security in our physical bodies; without them it is difficult to do many things in the world. However, we often do not realise how much security we have invested in our bodies until something goes wrong with them, until they are threatened by accident or disease. If you were paralysed after a road accident or had to have your legs amputated, what would it mean to you? Think about it for a moment. Some people survive the most horrendous physical damage with a spirit that is magnificent. For a Product-driven person, losing their physical faculties is perhaps the biggest threat.

Another area of security for Product types is the ability to protect themselves from assault. Unfortunately, it is a threat that many of us are having to consider more often. Some of us try to avoid putting ourselves at risk, others want to see increased police vigilance. For a Product type, however, the question is 'Can I look after myself?'

I was brought up in a pretty rough area and I suppose I've done well for myself. I know it's stupid but even now, whenever I meet another bloke, I find myself sizing him up immediately, asking, 'Could I sort him out if it came to it?'

30-year-old manual worker

Have you ever considered how you would respond in an assault situation? There are thousands of people engaged in various martial arts and self-defence activities aimed at enabling them to cope in such risk situations. (There are also those who are involved in the same activities for spiritual development, a completely different hilltop!) If you are involved in martial arts, you might ask what motivates your interest.

 Self-awareness questions

How much security do you place in being physically able?

Are you concerned about being able to defend yourself?

Status

Status is another of those words that has been used in a pejorative way in our culture. There is a common attitude towards status seekers, and a whole list of attributes and behaviours associated with it. Most of us need some form of status, some recognition that we are of value, even if it is never publicly acclaimed. We basically need to feel that we are worthy, and when that need is met, we feel a degree of satisfaction.

What gives people status in their own eyes of course comes back to individual hilltops: with some people it is their possessions, with others it is their intellectual prowess, and so on. We give status to what we personally value.

For a Product-driven person, status comes, predictably, from the physical aspects of life. Having a good body is extremely important. Keeping in shape is part of the body-consciousness we have if we identify with the Product drive. Fitness and health may be great motives for strenuous activity, but there are many people who also want to look good. For a Product type, the first thing (and perhaps the main thing) they take notice of when they meet someone else is their body.

 Self-awareness questions

What do you value about your physical abilities?

What status do you give to physical activities?

Think of someone who, in your eyes, has status. What gives them it?

Have you ever wondered why fitness clubs have sun-beds, saunas, etc.? Why do many people search out holidays where they can lie in a deck lounger for two weeks soaking up the sun?

For people who have a lot of Product drive, looking good and feeling good physically gives them status. Are you on a diet? If not, do you know people who are? Ask them why, and if they say 'To lose weight of course, I'm getting fat', then ask them why again. It will, in most cases, come down to self-image: looking and feeling good is important to them.

'But surely' some of you might say, 'we are conditioned into thinking that the stereotypical slim-waisted body is the symbol of perfection'. True, we agree, and in other times and in other cultures the conditioning leads to different ideals. But this could be an indication of just how powerful conditioning is when it connects with our own drives.

Self-awareness questions

How important is your body to you?

What do you do to make it look good?

How much notice do you take of other people's physique?

Use 3LT to explore your answers.

Another mark of status for Product types is physical prowess. Whatever the activity, there is lots of status attached to skill, suppleness, pure strength. Being the fastest runner, the hardest hitter, the world's strongest man or woman are all status symbols, whether in gymnastics or arm wrestling in the local pub. Even casual aerobic dance classes tend to be given levels of difficulty, and for Product types, it can be important to be in the most advanced class.

This of course brings us onto sex – a huge element in the Product drive. Sex is such a powerful part of this drive that it deserves a chapter to itself. We are not talking of sex as a security need or sexual prowess as a mark of status; although for many people it can be that. We are talking about the all-pervasive nature of sex that dominates a hilltop that is Product-driven. It is the one aspect of the Product drive that most people (not all) have an interest in.

Take almost any group of people, give them a while to get to know each other and, in a relatively short space of time, the subject of sex emerges. We find it often comes out in stories, jokes and repartee. It is an implicit and slightly taboo agenda that many people share.

To give you an idea of how it permeates our society, consider how much is sold using sex as the medium in film, video, books, magazines, and advertising for so many products. How many people do you know whose mind turns to sex at the slightest provocation, people who, given any opportunity, will see a double entendre in the most innocent remark? Be honest – how many times a day does sex enter your awareness?

For Product types, sex is a lens through which they see the world. Whether male or female, a member of the opposite sex is automatically viewed from a sexual angle.

Now all this may sound terribly sexist, and of course it is. When it comes to interacting with others, perceptions are often dominated by sexual impressions – no more, no less. If you work in a culture that has a high Product focus, then there is likely to be sex everywhere, if not in the form of pin-ups on the wall then in the language or humour.

Self-awareness questions

How interested in sex are you?
How often do you think of sex?
How strong is your sex drive?

Food

Food is of course essential to all of us, but it figures more highly in some people's lives than in others'.

There is a spectrum of attitudes towards food by people who have strong Product drives. On the one hand, as part of the health-conscious boom, healthy eating has become something of a fixation. Fresh food, organic food, cholesterol-free food, low sugar, low salt, high fibre – the list goes on and on. The move towards healthy eating has seen quite extraordinary attempts by marketing agencies to develop fat-free, additive-free, bio-conscious images for their products, attempting to appeal to people who want to look after their bodies.

On the other hand, many Product types do not actually go in for healthy eating, they go for bulk. The overriding principle for these people tends to be quantity, not quality – big helpings, second helpings, huge amounts of high-calorie foods and meat.

A few years ago we did some work in a training centre that had been divested from a large heavy engineering company to become a profit centre in its own right. It offered its own range of programmes and also residential facilities so that other organisations could run their own programmes there. Unfortunately, no-one seemed to have told the catering staff that they were no longer catering exclusively for a heavy engineering client group. The meals were enormous: layers of beef, pork and turkey stacked high with vegetables and potatoes, served by cheery middle-aged waitresses totally oblivious to any attempt to stop them piling on the helpings!

By the evening of the second day, one person, unable to cope with another assault, asked for a simple cheese salad, a request that was greeted with a puzzled look of slight disbelief, but nevertheless politely handled.

A few minutes later, the salad arrived – a huge plate of salad with what really must have been about a pound and a half of finely grated cheese stacked like a volcano in the middle of the plate!

For some people with a strong Product drive, the need to eat can at times override every other consideration. When travelling with a certain colleague we have on several occasions had to leave the motorway to search out 'fodder': the state of hunger needed immediate attention.

A very noticeable characteristic of Product types is often the way they eat. They do not usually pick or nibble, they wolf their food down. Have you ever looked up from an empty plate after sitting down for a meal to discover that others have hardly made an impression?

 Self-awareness questions

What are your favourite foods?

How much care do you take over what you eat?

What quantities do you consume?

How often do you eat simply to put something inside you?

Entertainment

We are looking at the Product drive from many different angles, hoping that you are exploring your own relationship with this particular drive. We have looked at the kinds of work that appeal to Product types, the leisure pursuits that you predictably find them engaged in and at what's important to them in their lives.

We cannot cover every activity and nuance of this, or any, of the drives, but we are building a picture of the core elements so that you can clearly identify the different drive states and use them as a map with which to understand yourself and other people.

Another useful clue for any of the types is to understand what entertains them, and why. When a Product type comes home from a hard day's work, he or she may not feel the need to go out for a run or dig the garden. Nevertheless, when sitting watching television, there are predictable programmes that will be of interest – the ones with high Product content.

Many people complain about the amount of sport on television, but a lot of it is watched by people who have an interest in Product-driven activity. Competition between two people or two teams can be compelling viewing for such a type. To them, the sight of two athletes who have endured pain and years of hard work to build their bodies to the peak of strength and fitness, with the will, determination and courage to put themselves on the line and risk severe damage in pursuit of their goal, is truly impressive. To others it is the height of savagery.

Apart from sport, there are the thrills and spills of the action movies: the fights, the chases, the blood and gore from certain directors, the macho movies, and war films. Why do you think *Rambo* and films of that ilk are so hugely popular? And of course every video shop has sex films in abundance – in all degrees of explicitness.

When it comes to humour, television spares us the worst Product type jokes, and offers instead the mild titillations of 'slap and tickle' comedy or the overt focus of the *Carry On* films. If you want to see the finest examples of Product-driven humour, go and see some of the 'blue' stand-up comics on the club circuit. Sexual jokes are their stock in trade, the more explicit the better. Gross jokes about any bodily function go down well, the thread throughout being a focus on the physical aspects of life.

 Self-awareness questions

What Product type of programmes or films do you watch?

Do you read any books that are 'action adventures'?

How much of your humour is Product-based?

Negative aspects

We have focused on the Product drive as a positive, healthy drive to nurture and nourish, to do productive work and manifest the capacities of the physical form. However, as we are all aware, there are people, events and behaviours in the world that are far from that – behaviours that are negative, destructive and disempowering. We understand them as negative expressions of the same drives that we are portraying, and we need to give them some attention if we are to understand them.

If a positive expression of the Product drive is care and nourishment of the body, then the negative expression is the abuse of it. There are many examples of people in our society who grossly overeat, or eat little else but junk food: the focus is not on the health and fitness of the body but on satiating hunger with huge servings of unhealthy food. Drinking excessively is also a negative expression of the Product drive: there are men and women (but probably more men) who are committed to eight pints of beer every night without fail – bulk liquid carriers! Lethargy and laziness are also expressions of bodily attachment – in this case to do nothing or as little with it as possible!

A more serious and damaging expression of the negative Product drive is physical violence. In childhood it may be playground bullying, in adulthood, assault, mugging, wife beating and murder.

The first line of defence for a Product type is very often physical attack. Have you ever found yourself in a situation where you felt you only had to say the wrong thing, or smile at the wrong time, or not smile at all, or do anything or nothing and the 'heavy' who was leering at you might just hit you?

In many countries, ball games have been ravaged by the violence of a hooligan element, people for whom fighting is a legitimate and, in the main, enjoyable activity for a Saturday afternoon. (There are other factors involved in this phenomenon which we will deal with when we discuss group identity as a drive, but clearly the Product drive features very strongly in the hooligan mentality.) Vandalism is another expression, using the Product drive to destroy and deface rather than build and create.

 ## Self-awareness questions

Do you express your Product drive in any negative ways?

Do you overeat?

Do you drink alcohol in large quantities?

Do you smoke?

Are you ever violent?

What is your opinion of the Product drive?

How do you view the Product type?

How do you relate to people like this?

What does that say about your own hilltop?

Use 3LT to explore your attitude to the Product drive.

We have by now given you enough of the feel of this drive state for you to be able to recognise it when you see it. What we encourage you to do now is reflect on the answers you have given to the self-awareness questions asked throughout this chapter, then make an intuitive assessment of how strong this drive is in you. Do you, for instance, feel no identification with this drive? Is it a drive that you virtually never engage in, or one you even avoid? Or do you relate strongly to it? Score yourself on the following scale:

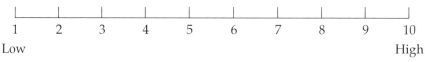

| 1 | 2 | 3 | 4 | 5 | 6 | 7 | 8 | 9 | 10 |

Low   High

We are not suggesting that you should know immediately how strong a part of your hilltop this drive is, although you may have a good idea. We would suggest that you suspend judgment for a while. After you have completed the other drive states you will then be in a position to judge its relative strength and predominance. Until then we are asking you to simply observe yourself in action and acknowledge what parts of your hilltop and your behaviour are covered by the Product aspect of the 7P map.

? ## Developing your Drives Profile – The Product Drive

What is your opinion of the Product drive?

How do you view the Product type?

How do you relate to people like this?

What does that say about your own hilltop?

Use 3LT to explore your attitude to the Product drive.

Reflect on the answers you have given to the self-awareness questions asked throughout this chapter, then make an intuitive assessment of how strong this drive is in you.

```
|      |      |      |      |      |      |      |      |      |      |
 1      2      3      4      5      6      7      8      9      10
Low                                                            High
```

Monitor your activities day by day and be aware of how much of what you say, think and do is a readout of this particular drive. Be prepared to modify your assessment in the light of what you discover in later drive chapters.

For now consider:

How much of a Product -driven person am I?

How much Product drive does my work demand?

How much Product drive do I satisfy outside work?

Summary

When you identify with the Product drive the things that are important to you are:

Physical activity, action, doing something

A need to produce something concrete

Food, diet, health, fitness

Bodily appearance, sex, physical prowess

Being stimulated physically

People who are strongly Product-driven are good at:

Getting on with the job

Working with physical things

Solving practical problems

Being pragmatic

Persevering with a task

Displaying stamina

At work you will find them doing things like:

Working with their hands

Manual labour

Skilled labour, e.g. machining, building, plastering, welding

The main industries for Product types are:

Engineering

Mining

Construction

Farming and fishing

Transportation

Outside of work, people with strong Product drives are often attracted to:

Sporting activity with a high physical content

Physical exertion

Doing practical things, e.g. home repair, gardening, car mechanics

Being active

Keeping fit and healthy

Looking good

Sex

CHAPTER 6

The People Drive

Key traits: *Friendship, caring, service, sense of belonging, acceptance, loyalty, conformity.*

In your life and your work, what importance do you place on getting on with people?

In many ways the people drive is the *glue* of our society. Whether in terms of national identity, community spirit or corporate loyalty, it is largely this drive that *holds people together.* At the core of a hilltop that is people-focused is the basic belief that caring and sharing with other people is the most important thing in life. If the Product drive is about the world of physical experience, the people drive is about the energy that flows between people in human interactions. It's not an activity that is important, it is the doing of it *together.*

Work

Work that fulfils the People drive is work that primarily involves dealing with others. We could argue that, with the exception of night watchmen and lighthouse keepers, all work involves dealing with people, and to a degree that is obviously true. In many cases, however, dealing with others is simply a means to an end. For those who satisfy their People drive in the work they do, interacting with other people is both a means *and* an end.

Work that provides this opportunity crosses a wide spectrum of occupations and industries. There is the huge service sector, staffed at the customer contact point by people who (hopefully) enjoy doing their best to help people. The next time you are in a hotel, ask the waiter or waitress what they like about working there – 90 per cent of the time you will get a response about liking the people they serve or work with. Airline ticketing agents get a special feeling of satisfaction when helping travellers.

If you examine some of the customer-care initiatives so prominent in recent years in management literature, you will find at the core a focus on dealing with people. One of the major factors in the success of the fast food chains, for example, is the importance they place on friendly, helpful service. In places that get it right you feel an informal welcoming atmosphere the moment you walk in. In places that get it wrong, you feel like an intrusion into an otherwise efficient operation.

The retail trade is another huge opportunity for work that satisfies the People drive. In the department store or the corner shop, the importance and satisfaction is in dealing with people. And, of course, the archetypal professions for this drive are the caring professions – nursing and welfare, social service and community work. The overriding principle that constrains industrial action in such professions is clearly the heartfelt need to care for those served.

Of course, not everyone in these fields could possibly be classed as People-driven. The distinction is exemplified in the difference traditionally cited between nurses and doctors, i.e. the nurse comforts and cares for the patient, the doctor cures the illness. Why is it that many doctors are regarded as having a poor bedside manner? We would suggest it comes down to individual hilltops: what is important for such doctors is medical problem solving, rather than giving tender loving care. For those with a strong People drive, care, empathy and compassion are the basis of good health care.

 ## Self-awareness questions

How much of your work involves you in dealing with people?

Is it an important aspect of your job?

Why is it important to you?

Within organisations

Satisfying the need to get on with people is by no means limited to the realm of customer contact. Many people who work within organisations find roles that satisfy this drive in the interactions within the workplace. The commercial or private sector equivalent to the caring professions is personnel and training. If you examine the motivation of many who work in these departments, the hilltop position is helping people in their job, career or development.

There are tens of thousands of people who work at monotonous, repetitive jobs in production capacities whose main enjoyment is the people they work alongside. The classic studies carried out in the 1950s on groups working together, and the Hawthorne studies, demonstrated the power of group identity so central to the People drive. Faced with boring, often mindless tasks, the way to improve morale and team spirit was to arrange work so that the people could interact with each other. There are many jobs where the skills, once mastered, can be put on automatic pilot, leaving the individual free to talk and socialise. The images of a component assembly line or a biscuit-packing conveyor process might be unattractive to many of us, but as a situation where you can socialise and have a laugh with friends it has great value.

Office work, the typing pool, catering and maintenance – the list of possible jobs for People-driven types is endless. The common theme is being part of a group, whatever the group is engaged in.

The People type

We would have to develop a compendium of careers to do full justice to all the possible roles in which you would find opportunities to satisfy the People drive. There are some company directors we know who have a lot of this drive within them, and it tends to be reflected in the culture of the organisations they lead. However, they tend to be relatively rare animals, for predominance of this drive leads predictably to a lack of focus on some of the others.

The People type – the person whose profile is dominated by this drive – has, like all the others, some predictable strengths and limitations. Of prime importance are people, good relationships and a sense of belonging. They like to get on with all people, feel part of an identifiable group and care for the people around them. They are often described as friendly helpers, and they readily take new co-workers under their wings.

Work is essentially seen as a place for social interaction, and a group of People-driven types working together can often resemble a party. We do not mean to imply that People types are not good workers – on the contrary, they are usually very competent, responsible and loyal and will always do the best they can. What it does imply is that they are not usually inner-directed and often need direction from above.

People types make good team workers. Their natural style is one of co-operation. They have the knack of developing good group atmospheres, smiling through adversity and cheering people up (unless you have no People drive yourself, in which case they can grate terribly!).

If you are fortunate enough to have a strong People type in your team, even the direst of situations can seem less grey. They are always the ones to inject a bit of humour or light-heartedness, often seeming almost incapable of taking life too seriously. They are natural optimists.

Being a People type essentially means occupying an emotional world, not a rational one. It is a hilltop that feels for others rather than thinks about things in any depth.

> *Of course I care about what's happening in Ethiopia and places like that. I could cry every time I see those awful pictures, but I can't think about it all the time. It would drive me mad.*
>
> 28-year-old office worker

Positive People types are full of vitality, and love a good laugh with a group of friends. If you have such a thing as an annual company social event, they are the ones you will see having an uninhibited song and dance party. To the horror of many other types, they are the first on the dance floor, and are always the ones to drag you, protesting, onto your feet to join the fun! They work from a basic principle of 'The more we are together the happier we shall be!'

If you manage People types it is important to recognise the need they have for company. If you want to get the least out of them, give them a job that isolates them. The effects will be disastrous.

 ## Self-awareness questions

How much of a social animal are you at work?
How many colleagues do you class as friends?
What time do you spend chatting with them?
Use 3LT to explore your answers.

Another interesting aspect of People types we have noticed is their ability for work that involves dexterity – not the heavy physical work of the Product type but work that requires nimble fingers, a fine touch. A lot of them are good at getting machines to run smoothly, but if you ask them how they do it they almost certainly could not explain. It is as though at one level they feel energies between people, at another they feel the energies in the materials or machines they are working with – and a little tweak here and there will do the trick.

Limitations

The strengths of People types can also be their limitations. They are so concerned with maintaining nice atmospheres that they really do not like upsetting people or rocking the boat. The selflessness of always volunteering for the worst task in a group effort becomes an inability to put themselves first when they need to.

Assertiveness is a difficult issue for many People types. 'No' is a very difficult word for these people because it means refusing to do something, refusing to help, refusing a request. (It is even worse when they are asked nicely – a tip for all of you who need to influence People types!) The only time you will see a People type assert him or herself is usually on someone else's behalf. 'It doesn't matter, I don't want to make a fuss', and 'I don't mind, I'm happy to go along with what the group decides', are typical People type statements.

A few months ago, we were running a two-day workshop around the 7Ps of drive. After lunch, one of the participants came up and asked if it would be possible to leave a little early to catch a certain train, immediately backing up the request with an apology and an offer to stay if it would upset the group working (even though it meant a two-hour wait for a later train). When we pointed out the People drive in his request he decided to try again more assertively: 'I will need to leave early this afternoon to catch the train home (pause), if that's OK with you!'

As managers, People types are faced with a predictable dilemma. Their friendly, participative style of management develops good working relationships where they are often perceived as caring and empathetic. However, the same qualities make it difficult for them to discipline people or be clearly directive when they need to. It is something that many hate doing, a distasteful aspect of the role. At the worst extreme they can become ineffectual because of it.

Self-awareness questions

How easy is it for you to assert yourself?

How often do you 'let things go' rather than upset people?

Is being a 'friendly helper' important? If so, why?

There are certain kinds of tasks that People types are predictably weak at if they do not have access to some of the other drive states. One is planning. Not the planning that involves common sense – e.g. organising an activity or event – for that, many of them are excellent, their vitality and sociability making them good at sorting out tasks and getting them done. It is the kind of planning that involves abstract concepts and models that they are not good at.

As we said a little earlier, the People drive is an emotional drive, not a rational one. It is very difficult for a People type to find any meaning or relevance in abstractions – statistics, graphs, theoretical frameworks belong in another world as far as they are concerned. They simply cannot relate.

People types tend not to be good at making decisions, particularly unilateral decisions. Because of their need to include others, not upset people, to see other people's points of view, they often reach a point where they literally do not know what to do for the best.

Another related factor is the belief held by most People types that someone higher up the organisation will sort things out. They tend to lack the internal authority needed to decide the proper course of action.

 Self-awareness questions

How comfortable are you with abstract data?

How comfortable are you in leading other people?

Who do you look to for direction?

Use 3LT to explore your answers.

The overriding need to belong, to identify with a group, leads People types to invest a lot of energy in conforming to the norms of their particular group. One of the very worst punishments for such people is being set apart, or singled out or isolated. For many of us, being ostracised or simply not 'fitting in' is perhaps no big deal. For a People type it is the single most important aspect of their life.

We once met a highly-skilled factory worker who had been offered promotion to supervisor frequently, and had repeatedly turned it down. The underlying reason that came out in interviews was that he could not put himself in a position 'above' his workmates.

Loyalty to the group, presenting a united front, can be a commendable position – but it is fraught with dangers. One is that, with many groups, individuals conform to a working regime often far below their individual potential. How often have you heard stories of children at school suppressing their innate capacities so they do not stand out as different from the rest of their classmates? Much research has clearly demonstrated the subtle power of the group to set output targets below that which any individual in the group could achieve. Outperforming the rest of the group and thereby exceeding the group norm is subject to the heaviest censure.

The biggest danger – and the one that holds most difficulty for an organisation – is the membranes that develop around groups. Once a group identity is established it serves to separate the group from other groups and a 'them and us' mentality emerges. What predictably develops is a series of perceptions and attitudes towards other groups that often has little basis in reality – a group hill-top.

This inter-group phenomenon is one of the major factors in the informal structure within all organisations, i.e. how things actually get done in companies as opposed to how they should get done. In organisations that have large inter-group difficulties, co-ordinating processes can be a constant battle: Sales will not talk to Production, Planning sees Personnel as such and such, etc. Getting the people within an organisation to identify themselves as one large group has challenged many leading thinkers of the last decades.

The 'them and us' mentality is not necessarily confined to the nuances of any particular organisational structure – it can come right down to which coffee club you belong to, where you sit to eat lunch, or which clique you are involved in. And unfortunately, in our experience, it is predominantly the People types that feel – and often feed – those separations. Other people and other groups can very easily become targets for gossip – 'I will be friends, help and care for you. . . if you're one of us'.

Self-awareness questions

Which groups do you identify with at work?
What does your group think of the others around you?
How much do you engage in inter-group rivalry or gossip?

Leisure interests

The main focus of all People type activity is socialising.

If you ask a Product type what is important to them it will be activity, health, etc. If you ask the same question of a People type it will be friends. Leisure time for these people is to be spent doing things with their group of friends. Whatever the activity, it is primarily a vehicle for socialising.

People types love the energy and vitality generated when people are having fun together, when the conversation flows freely and the barriers come down.

There are many different attitudes to traditional times of celebration such as birthdays, Christmas, Chanukah, or the New Year. Some people see them as a waste of time, a commercialised ritual etc. To People types, however, they are high spots of the calendar, along with the summer holiday (which is also likely to be taken with a group of friends). These are the times when we can all get together and have a good time with the group or groups we identify with – our family, friends, neighbours etc. It is a time when we can show we care.

 Self-awareness questions

How much time do you like to spend socialising?
What kinds of things do you do with your friends?
What does New Year mean to you?
What do birthdays mean to you?
Use 3LT to explore your answers.

Belonging

If you live in a town or city that issues a local directory of clubs and societies, spend an hour browsing through the vast range that proliferates within your community. There are groups, clubs and societies that you will have never heard of before – the range is truly remarkable. Every evening, all over the world, countless groups get together to pursue their own particular interests. Whatever the activity, if you ask a People type what they get from doing it, they will tell you in some form or other that it is the *social* element that is important. They may have a strong interest in the activity itself, but highest on the scale of benefits is meeting with other people. As we have said, it is not the activity that is of prime importance, it is the doing of it together.

The People drive is particularly important in developing and maintaining community spirit. People types have a strong need to identify with a community of some sort. This may be the extended family, or the street where they live or the neighbourhood. One of the pleasures of many people's lives is to be able to walk to the local shops, cafes or pubs and say hello to familiar faces. Why? Because this makes us feel that we belong somewhere. If you shop locally, do you notice people who bump into each other on the street corner or in the supermarket, and are there for 20 minutes chatting away, oblivious to others? They are not usually discussing world affairs but the latest People-driven news and gossip about people they know, what's happening locally, who's doing what, etc.

For People types, community identity can extend to any group they feel affiliated with – a club, society, village, town, city, county, even a nation. When enlightened planners knock down inner-city slums to build cities in the sky, they destroy the social fabric of many communities. It took us a long time to discover that once you remove the caring heart of a society, it dies. People types can cope with the majority of living conditions; what they cannot cope with is isolation in little boxes with no chance to interact.

Unfortunately, the same inter-group phenomenon found within organisations exists in the wider world also. Every district of a city has a set of stereotyped assumptions laid on its inhabitants by the rest.

Where you live, is there a common perception of a nearby community, province or country that has people who are a bit odd, snobbish, or perhaps rough? Some people in the north think that people in the south are X, Y and Z, and vice versa.

 Self-awareness questions

Where do you belong?
What groups do you feel part of?
How strong is your need to belong?
Use 3LT to explore your answers.

Another aspect of community that is important to many People types is community work. There are many who willingly give their time to help others less fortunate than themselves, or work hard to put something back into the community they belong to. Look at the wealth of good work that is done by local voluntary associations, by people who care about where they live and doing something for people within their community.

Security

People types, predictably, find a lot of security in the friends and groups they feel involved with. They feel secure and can endure many personal tragedies if they have friends that they can share their troubles with. And of course they get terribly upset if a friend lets them down. Loyalty and trust are key elements in such relationships. Have you ever had your feelings hurt by not being invited to a friend's party, not being sent a card on a special occasion or by a friend not keeping in touch with you?

People types will go to great lengths to remain part of a group they are involved with, and this need for inclusion is often very transparent in young people as they struggle to find an identity. They have to wear the right clothes, use the group language, develop the right attitudes and be interested in the same activities as others in the group. Members of gangs often have to actively demonstrate their commitment to membership by wearing a badge or doing something daring or downright dangerous. Of course, as adults we may have achieved a degree of subtlety in our approach, but if we examine what we do to belong, the behaviour is probably still there.

 Self-awareness questions

How much do you value friends?
What is it that you value in belonging?
What would cause you to break with friends?

Another area where People types place their security is in the 'powers that be'. In modern society much of the pain and difficulty of life has been taken out of our hands: 'they' bury our dead, cure our illnesses, catch and punish our criminals and protect our safety. Many People types have undying faith in the powers that be to solve our problems, stemming basically from the need to have leaders whom they can follow and trust to come up with the answers. For example, you might hear, 'Global warming? There are some very clever people up there, they won't let it happen'. (Or will they?)

People types also place a lot of security in their community. If they feel that the fabric of their community is threatened, for example by government legislation or local council planning, and if enough of them feel the threat, they will mobilise community energy to protest. Many People types cannot get too excited by world events or national issues, but if there is a direct threat to their community, they will put their faith and their energy into people power.

Entertainment

We have already spent time detailing the socialising need in some depth, so how else do People types gain their entertainment? For People types, entertainment must create an emotional thrill. Television 'soaps' have a large People-driven audience and we suggest this is for two basic reasons.

One is that they are all about the intrigue, happenings and gossip in a close community. The other is that you can talk and speculate for hours about them with your friends the next day! True, we have not done empirical research on this, but if you know people who are avid viewers (presuming you are not), then ask them what it is they enjoy about them.

Generally speaking, what appeals to People types is light entertainment –

soaps, sitcoms, quiz shows, variety and chat shows are likely to be the fodder of an evening's viewing. They are programmes which do not ask you to think, reflect, enquire or be outraged, simply to be entertained. With reading, the focus is the same – it has to be light, almost always fiction, and with the buzz of emotional stimulation.

Self-awareness questions

Which of the above-mentioned types of television programme do you watch?

If you watch any, what do you enjoy about them?

If not, why not?

Use 3LT to explore your answers.

Negative aspects

We hope, as with all the types, that we have presented a positive image of the People drive. They are the salt of the earth; they put the social in society. Without this drive, we would have little that we could consider to be community at any level. They are the caring heart of our society.

We have already alluded to some of the more negative expressions of this type with the inter-group phenomenon. The most negative aspect is prejudice: 'If you do not conform to my group norms, come from the right place or speak with the right accent then you are not one of us.'.

It may be mildly expressed, as when a stranger moves into a tight-knit community and undergoes a gradual process of acceptance, or it may take an extreme form of group prejudice. Being of a different colour, sex, or sexual preference may, in the eyes of a People type, define you as 'other', meaning not one of *them*.

This, of course, comes back to the notion that each of us believes we are right in how we see the world and how we live our lives. When a People type can find others whose hilltops are close to his or hers, then his or her beliefs are reinforced.

The basis for prejudice can be virtually anything. Some experiments carried out in American schools demonstrated the frightening power of group identity. Students were segregated on the basis of eye colour, and told that research indicated that those with brown eyes were intellectually and socially inferior to those who had blue eyes. Such simple differentiation generated strong feelings, perceptions and conflicts that were only diffused by revealing to the students the nature of the experiment and the innate potential for prejudice.

Developing your Drives Profile – The People Drive

What is your opinion of the People drive?

How do you view the People type?

How do you relate to people like this?

What does that say about your own hilltop?

Use 3LT to explore your attitude to the People drive.

Reflect on the answers you have given to the self-awareness questions asked throughout this chapter, then make an intuitive assessment of how strong this drive is in you.

Low   High

Monitor your activities day by day and be aware of how much of what you say, think and do is a readout of this particular drive. Be prepared to modify your assessment in the light of what you discover in later drive chapters.

For now consider:

How much of a People-driven person am I?

How much People drive does my work demand?

How much People drive do I satisfy outside work?

Summary

The following things are important when you identify with the People drive:

Friendship, caring and support

A need to belong to a group

A busy social life

Conforming to group expectations

Laughter, fun and vitality

Those who are strongly People-driven are good at:

Getting on with others

Friendly, efficient customer care

Working as part of a team

Developing good working atmospheres

Playing their part responsibly

Seeing the best in others

You will find People types:

Working in a service capacity

Working as part of a team effort

Doing skilled work e.g. machining, typing, component assembly

Main industries are:

Service

Retail

Financial services

Health and social services

Community and welfare

Outside work, people with strong People drives are often attracted to:

Activity with a high interpersonal content

Belonging to clubs and societies

Doing things for others

Being one of the group

Maintaining a healthy social life

Having a laugh

Having emotional thrills

CHAPTER 7

The Process Drive

Key traits: *Intellectual and perceptual stimulation, research and analysis, change, novelty and variety, self-expression, being different, unconventionality, adaptability.*

As a label, the Process Drive is not as self-explanatory as those of some of the other drives.

At one level we are physical bodies, simply bone and muscle. At another level we are social animals, gathering together in groups, nourished by the emotional comfort and caring that such belonging provides. At the level of the Process drive, we are a human information processing system.

Have you ever considered how much information you process? Every second of your waking life, whether you are walking down the street, shopping in a crowded store, or driving your car, you are bombarded with information.

 ### Self-awareness exercise

Stop reading for one minute and focus on the range of information that you can perceive:

- bodily sensations,
- sounds,
- smells and tastes, and
- visual perceptions.

What about thoughts and feelings?

How much can you become aware of?

The ability to process information is one of the essential functions of all living organisms, be they plant, insect, or animal. At a very simple level, for example, an amoeba may experience light information, process it and respond by moving towards it.

At a more complex level, we all use this ability to make sense of and respond to the stimulations of everyday life. Whether finding our way through an unfamiliar town or reading about new ideas, we are constantly absorbing information, interpreting it and adding it to our pool of experience.

Processing information involves having some sort of perceptual stimulation and an intellect with which to chop up the experience to make sense of it. For people who have a strong Process drive, the processing of information in the form of life experience is more than an essential function – the act itself becomes a meaningful part of their hilltop and one that dictates much of their behaviour.

The Process type

People who have the Process drive as the predominant drive in their hilltop seek to fulfil their primary values in many different ways. They are people who constantly seek out new ideas, new information or new ways of looking at things. They are people who will often try something totally new simply to experience it. They are the people who naturally thrive on change and the stimulation and excitement that it can bring. They love to work on novel projects or with unusual ideas and to feel free to express themselves in whatever way they choose.

Work

The ideal work for a Process type involves the intellect in a stimulating and engaging way. They love nothing more than the challenge of making sense of a complex mass of data, or an intricate and intriguing problem. It allows them the opportunity to practice the processing skills of analysis and research.

Science is a great attraction to Process types. It really seems to matter little which of the many branches you examine – the laboratories of the world are brimming with such people. Whether they are on field study monitoring the movement of Scottish salmon in their migratory cycle, analysing statistical data from clinical tests or experimenting on the edges of particle physics, the stimulation is the same. It is the sense of discovery, the intellectual stimulation of finding out, and the experience of finding something new, that is the great reward.

Within industry, they are to be found in research and development laboratories – back-room boffins who spend years setting up intricate tests to analyse stress fractures in metals or generating thousands of biological experiments looking for possible new strains.

For many Process types, the Information Technology industry is the modern place to be. There are almost infinite possibilities for a lively mind in the computing world. People speak of getting hooked or addicted to it.

Process people may not be the ones responsible for a new original idea – that is often the realm of another type – but they are the ones who do the intellectual spadework to turn the idea into a working product.

Self-awareness questions

How much of your work involves analysis or research?

What do you enjoy about these activities?

How important is intellectual stimulation to you in your work?

Use 3LT to explore your answers.

The old saying that 'Variety is the spice of life' is certainly true for the Process type. Some people may find this difficult to match with the image of a computer programmer – someone apparently doing the same thing repeatedly. It is important to realise, however, that variety in this case comes from the stimulation of different problems and different challenges (remember no two computer programmes are the same!).

Unlike People types, who will happily do routine work as long as they have social interaction, for Process types (who hate routine), the work itself has to be interesting, or at least varied.

An enormous number of jobs appeal to Process types. There are many in training, for example – an area that offers new theories and techniques combined with a captive audience for the expression of those ideas.

Process types are often attracted to working in project teams or task forces that are charged with finding new solutions to old problems. They are natural change agents, working within organisations to bring in new ideas or ways of moving the organisation forward. They find excitement in sitting in meetings, playing with possibilities, turning things upside-down, exploring other perspectives.

If you are not of the Process persuasion yourself, it is easy to perceive them as intellectual butterflies, flitting excitedly from one idea to the next with very little substance to their words. For Process types, being identified as a lateral thinker is one of life's great accolades.

 Self-awareness questions

How important is variety in your work? Why?

How often do you get excited by new ideas?

How much of your time do you spend trying to change things?

Use 3LT to explore your answers.

Change is extremely important to Process types. Whether it is minute local variance or the kind of massive socio-political changes that have recently taken place in Eastern Europe, change is stimulation.

For the majority of Process types we have met, change seems inextricably wedded to another core value, freedom. By that we mean intellectual freedom and individual rights; the freedom to express oneself in thought, word and deed without the threat of censure. Process types have a strong need to express themselves and their ideas, beliefs and values.

Other work that attracts them is that which provides the opportunities for such self-expression. The entertainment industry and the media attract lots of Process types: these fast-moving and therefore stimulating environments offer great opportunities for self-expression.

Process type entertainers are the ones who have something to say, a statement to make about their beliefs. Alternative comedy is a good example. Street theatre and festivals are likely places to see Process type comedy in action. And musically, there are lots of Process types telling the world what they think. Rap music is an excellent example of using entertainment as a vehicle for delivering a message.

Process types love intellectual argument and debate. They are the people who will want to discuss and dissect any ideas or suggestions you have. They are the people who will disagree or take an opposing view in order to generate a debate. Why? Because it is intellectually stimulating to take things to pieces and analyse them. It is also important to realise that this is how Process types *learn.* They take things to pieces in order to understand them. Intellectual debate is a means by which they test their opinions and arguments in a stimulating way.

Academia is the natural home of the Process type – not in the form of the staid old professor who thinks he or she knows everything about a particular subject (although at one time they too may have been a Process type), but the young enthusiastic lecturer, researcher or student.

Many of you who are reading this may have experienced life at college, polytechnic or university. Do you remember the papers you had to write comparing and contrasting differing points of view, the seminars where the lecturer would dissect the undissectable, the long nights arguing about politics, religion and any other contentious subject matter?

It is difficult to imagine an environment more conducive to young Process types than the campus, and indeed some Process types become eternal students, always delving into new areas of study, new paths that stimulate their need to learn and discover.

Self-awareness questions

How often do you express your ideas, views and beliefs?

How often do you engage in debate and intellectual discussions?

Use 3LT to explore your answers.

Limitations

We have already described a common perception of Process types as being intellectual butterflies. While they have lots of enthusiasm and energy for new ideas and a high level of cognitive capacity, they also tend to have little in the way of follow through. Once the initial stimulation and excitement of an idea has died down, they often find it difficult to maintain interest in the more 'mundane' tasks that naturally follow. They therefore tend to be seen as lacking the weight or commitment to follow an idea all the way through to implementation.

Many Process types have difficulty working within a system. Their need for change and stimulation will often lead them into being the non-conformists within an organisation. They are the ones who find ways to buck the system, to develop idiosyncratic working methods that may not be better, simply different. They can be the bane of a manager's life because of it, and when challenged will always need the manager to produce a logical, justifiable argument, and to be given a chance to express their own position.

Leisure interests

Outside your work environment the same basic drives hold true. The primary drives for intellectual and perceptual stimulation, for change, freedom and self-expression, find many outlets.

Process types need to feel *different*, not the biggest or the best, but different. The drive for conformity displayed by most People types is anathema to them. They are likely to have interests in the unusual, whatever sphere of activity they choose. If they are interested in theatre or cinema, for example, it will tend to be the more avant-garde that attracts them. Experimental theatre companies and political theatre groups draw Process types, as do small independent cinemas showing films that never make general release.

If the interest is music then it is often in the form of a specialism – Cajun music, Tibetan Nose flute, Stockhausen, techno, rap, diatonic, etc. Of course, once it becomes popular, the Process type loses enthusiasm and moves to the next new wave.

Self-awareness questions

What kinds of theatre or cinema appeal to you?

How unusual is your taste in music or literature?

How important is being different to you?

Use 3LT to explore your answers.

If a Process type's interests involve physical activity, they are the classic explorers. They explore the different, the unusual. They are the people who will travel the more remote areas of the world, meeting new cultures, expanding their experience of life, having new adventures. Many of the documentaries we see of expeditions are the stories of Process types: they canoe the wild waters of the Himalayas, hang glide over the Pyrenees, ride motorbikes across the Sahara, and climb Norwegian fjord walls. They are not the package holidaymakers of the Costa Del Sol, they are the overland trekkers to Nepal, Africa, Thailand. The Hippies of the 1960s included many young Process types dropping out of conventional society and doing their own thing.

In the last decade or more, there has been growing interest in inner exploration, what we lovingly call 'Inward Bound'. Experiential learning groups are highly attractive to Process types. Everything, from Primal Scream to Transpersonal Psychology, and Creative Dance Therapy to Sexuality Awareness Groups, provides a rich source of stimulation and learning for these people.

 Self-awareness questions

What ways do you find for expressing yourself?

What do you explore?

What do you gain from doing these things?

Use 3LT to explore your answers.

Process types are great collectors – but not in the sense of wealth or priceless works of art (indeed many would reject such materialism). They are great collectors of the unusual: the status of an object is rarely its price but is in its being different, out of the ordinary, even bizarre. Furniture, ornaments, books, teacup handles – the more unusual it is the better. The music collection of a Process type may be impossible to categorise into this taste or that. It will usually be completely eclectic, providing an historical glimpse of the range of new music of the period, or it will have a strange mix of performers that few people have heard of.

Process types also collect experiences. One of the greatest benefits for them of travelling, for example, is collecting unique experiences that can be recounted in story form. It is not a case of one-upmanship, simply that experiences are what make life worthwhile.

 Self-awareness questions

What things do you collect?

How unusual or different are they?

What are peak experiences for you?

Use 3LT to explore your answers.

The primary focus for socialising when a group of Process types get together is some form of intellectual stimulation or self-expression, perhaps in the form of an intellectual debate. If you frequent the traditional student pubs in your area you will find Process types engaging in debate or argument, picking holes in the various positions held, even though there may be common aims, values and beliefs. They love social activity which stimulates discussion. One noticeable trait of such people is their ability to collect and retain a wealth of information, facts, and data – a store from which to generate discussion. Whatever the subject, a Process type will have something to say about it, some perspective to put on the table to argue about. They can, on the one hand, use their intellect to cut through arguments to reveal the 'truth'. On the other, they can be seen as devil's advocates – generating points of view at random, only to knock them down.

One major area where all these Process drives come together is politics. Process types have a natural affinity with processes for political change. The desire for change usually (but not always) pushes them into positions that are to the left of the political spectrum.

We are not talking about party politics, as though all socialists were Process types. (Indeed, there are as many 'natural conservatives' within labour parties around the world as in other parties.) We are talking more of political action around the fringes of party politics. If you look at the people who are active in the promotion of various change and individual freedom causes, you will find Process types in the majority of cases.

We are not saying that everyone who supports such groups is by definition a

Process type. What we observe is that the majority of people we see demonstrating their commitment to such causes by marching, protesting or vociferously expressing their opinions are, in the main, Process types. Indeed, if it were not for them, many social changes would have been much slower in coming – they are the grass roots change agents in our society.

The same phenomenon seems to occur in local communities. While it may be the People types who feel the need to belong and have a good community spirit, it is often the Process types who initiate and are involved in running community action groups.

 Self-awareness questions

What is your political position?

What beliefs do you base that position on?

How much does change and individual freedom figure in those beliefs?

Use 3LT to explore your answers.

Security

A Product type places security in having a healthy body and the ability to do things; a People type in having the support of a social group when times get hard. Process types place their security primarily in their capacity to change and their ability to adapt.

For many people, hitch-hiking across your continent with nothing more than a rucksack and a very small amount of money is quite a threatening proposition. Would you do it? Throwing up a steady job without seriously contemplating the future first is something that many of us would resist. Would you?

 Self-awareness questions

Where do you place your security?

How willingly do you embrace change?

How adaptable do you feel yourself to be?

Use 3LT to explore your answers.

For Process types security is not in the status quo, it is in their ability to manage changing situations. In fact, for many, fixation is the ultimate threat. Being locked into a single path with no opportunity to escape – for instance, a career in which the next 30 years can be mapped out – is, to them, a truly horrifying thought. It is often the same within relationships. Many Process types find real difficulty in committing themselves to an ongoing relationship that vows to be forever. Indeed, settling down is the ultimate abandonment of Process type values.

> A few years ago, we were working with a group of young managers on a self-development programme. After the first few days, having learned some basic skills including the Three Level Technique, one young man clearly signalled some distress: 'You don't need anyone else to practise this technique with – you can use it on yourself, can't you?' What had disconcerted him was the discovery that over the last six years he had 'sold out' on the principles he espoused so vigorously as a student, without recognising the transition. From a young single graduate he had become a married home-owner and father of two children – a real 'Mr Conformity'.

Age

There is an apparent age factor with the Process drive that you may have felt implied in the description so far. This drive first blossoms in youth – most of our educational system is in fact geared towards its development. Examinations, IQ tests, and higher education all focus on the development of the intellect and critical faculties (often to the exclusion of some of the others).

The archetype of this age is the rebellious teenager who needs to test the boundaries of parental or teacher control, or the student who is more than willing to challenge the authority of his or her lecturers in intellectual duels.

Youth culture and street fashion is driven largely by young Process types attempting to carve out their individuality. In the 1960s in England it was the Mods (the Rockers were mostly Product types), then the Hippies, and the late 1970s and early 1980s saw the emergence of the Punk generation. Now we have such a variety that it is difficult to generalise (or are we now too old to make distinctions?). What do you perceive as the emerging youth culture of this millennium?

Later in life, the archetype becomes the traveller, the adventurer, the pioneer; the person who has been to most places, lived life to the full, and had a lot of very interesting experiences in such a relatively young life. 'I finished university and took off abroad for a few years, maybe had 20 jobs, all of them different. Worked as a road sweeper in Bangkok before becoming a deckhand on a charter yacht heading for Australia' is a typical thumbnail sketch.

? Self-awareness questions

What does 'settling down' mean to you?
How varied has your career been?
How often do you feel the need for change?
Use 3LT to explore your answers.

As Process types get older there is, for many, a natural dilemma. The drive for change and stimulation is often overshadowed by taking on responsibilities, a partner, commitments, etc. Some simply refuse to change and in fact fixate on the values and beliefs formed in their earlier years. Others manage to find a lifestyle that supports many of their Process type values: one which includes alternatives to the traditional nuclear family, for example, or the traditional nine-to-five job. Some manage to remain young-minded and free-thinking even into old age.

For example, John Peel, the longest-running radio DJ in England, was tipped to be the first of the original bunch likely to be weeded out. He was a little too radical for the BBC in earlier days. Some people lately have challenged him on his continued interest in the modern pop scene, intimating that there is nothing original in today's music. Peel's response is that, after 20 years, he is still as keen as ever to get to the studio to see what new releases or demos have arrived every day. He has simply continued to change and has not succumbed to fixating on a particular musical style of the past.

Status

We give status to what we admire. Predictably, Process types give status to the people who live out the values of the Process type hilltop. There is status in being intellectually agile, in games, in discussion, and in being able to generate piercing arguments. There is status in being widely travelled or having led an interesting and varied life.

Process types see particular status in being a rebel, a non-conformist, fighting the system to bring about some kind of change. Che Guevara, for example, is one of the most enduring heroes of the Process type. On a non-political level, being unconventional, unusual or downright outrageous brings status to a Process type: it is the commitment to be different that is important, whether in ideology, perspective or behaviour.

Process types often want to dress differently from others. Even within an established company culture, those small differences are often noticeable – a slightly outrageous tie, unusual spectacles, something that is an expression of individuality.

 Self-awareness questions

What Process qualities do you admire?

What do you give status to?

How much do you need to be a non-conformist?

Use 3LT to explore your answers.

Humour

Process type humour usually has an intellectual base, often taking comedy sketches into the realms of the absurd. *Monty Python's Flying Circus* ushered onto our screens a new era of humour, developing a cult following among Process types and setting a genre that many have since followed.

Political humour almost always has its roots in the Process drive. The so-called alternative comedy circuit takes as its subject matter the conventional attitudes towards racism, sexism, equality etc. and paints a different perspective on them. You will not find the usual topics within the repertoire of a Process humourist, or if you do they will be turned upside down as the punch-line pokes fun at the prejudices within our society.

 Self-awareness questions

What are your favourite comedy programmes?

What humour makes you laugh?

What leaves you cold?

Negative aspects

When a Process type becomes negative, he or she can become the professional cynic. The intellect is used as a cutting tool to dissect and destroy enthusiasm and hope. Combined with a cutting tongue, they become weapons with which to intellectually attack or undermine others.

Some feel constrained and resentful towards society in general and authority figures in particular. They develop a strong counter-dependency and will be drawn into confrontation and conflict at the slightest provocation. Driven to extremes, they become society's rebels, challenging and rejecting the status quo, even if it means breaking the law to demonstrate their beliefs and further their causes.

On a more individual basis, many disillusioned Process types find their mental and perceptual stimulation in drugs.

Developing your Drives Profile – The Process Drive

What is your opinion of the Process drive?

How do you view the Process type?

How do you relate to people like this?

What does that say about your own hilltop?

Use 3LT to explore your attitude to the Process drive.

Reflect on the answers you have given to the self-awareness questions asked throughout this chapter, and then make an intuitive assessment of how strong this drive is in you.

| 1 | 2 | 3 | 4 | 5 | 6 | 7 | 8 | 9 | 10 |

Low   High

Monitor your activities day by day and be aware of how much of what you say, think and do is a readout of this particular drive. Be prepared to modify your assessment in the light of what you discover in later drive chapters.

For now consider:
• How much of a Process-driven person am I?
• How much Process drive does my work demand?
• How much Process drive do I satisfy outside my work?

Summary

Important things to Process-driven people are:

- Intellectual and perceptual stimulation
- Research and analysis
- Change, novelty and variety
- Self-expression and adaptability
- Being different and unconventional

Those who are strongly Process-driven are good at:

- Research and analysis
- Scientific rigour
- Working on novel projects
- Trying out new ideas, initiating change
- Expressing ideas articulately

Professionally they often:

- Work in a change agent capacity
- Work with lots of variety and stimulation
- Work as part of a new projects team
- Do cognitive work, e.g. research, analysis, computer programming, presenting, academic work

Main industries are:

- Science and technology
- Information Technology
- Education
- Entertainment and media
- Retail involving technical knowledge e.g. specialist broadcasting, digital media

Outside work, people with strong Process drives are often attracted to:

- Unusual activities
- Exploration and discovery
- Fringe activities
- Political and civil rights issues
- Being ahead of the crowd
- Non-conformity

CHAPTER 8

The Power Drive

Key traits: *Energy, commitment, emotional attachment, recognition, success, being influential, risk-taking, challenge, competition, acquisition, status, control.*

When people describe someone as having lots of drive, it is usually the Power drive they are referring to. 'Go out and get what you want', 'Make something of yourself' and 'Leave your mark in the world' are all exhortations of the Power drive. The enterprise culture that has been fostered in many countries is a clear appeal to us all to be more Power-driven.

We hope that by now, your appreciation of the different drives we all have is broadening from this somewhat limited perspective, and that you can appreciate that what some people want, or want to make of themselves, has nothing to do with the Power drive whatsoever.

Being Power-driven is essentially a question of identity. We all have a sense of identity, we are aware of our own existence. It is one of the characteristics that separates us from other animals. This sense of identity develops as we grow and interact with the world, from a new-born baby seemingly unable to distinguish itself as an entity separate from its surroundings, to a mature adult clearly conscious of many layers of complexity both in itself and its environment.

Along with this sense of identity develops a sense of self-esteem, for we often value or judge our own abilities and achievements. Much of our sense of self-worth comes from the recognition or judgment of our parents, peers and teachers during our formative years. The Power drive is about self-esteem – it is the drive to recognise and value ourselves as unique entities in the world, to feel that we are 'someone' rather than 'no-one', to be able to affect situations in which we find ourselves rather than feel powerless.

Why do some people go to the lengths they do to succeed? Where does the energy that impels them come from? There are many wonderful examples of people who have found the will and commitment to succeed in achieving a goal that they have set themselves. Some reach the top of their chosen field, or become a household name. Others commit all their energy to amassing resources in the form of businesses, money or political influence. We propose that the basic force behind the Power drive is the need to feel that we exist.

The direct relationship of the Power drive to the common perception of the ego deserves some attention. Phrases such as, 'He's got a big ego' or 'She's on a massive ego-trip' or 'It gave me a great ego-boost' are all pointing to this sense of identity or self-worth. Unfortunately, most of the references we hear to the ego have some negative connotations, as though having an ego is inherently bad. Developing a healthy ego is the goal of much personal development: people learn to assert themselves positively, to respect and value their own rights and the rights of others, to accept challenge and risks.

Our understanding of the ego is as a membrane around each unique hilltop that distinguishes 'Me and Mine' from everything else that is 'Not Me and Mine'. It is a membrane that we create that includes as 'Me' the things in life that we feel to be important, the things we feel emotionally attached to. There is nothing wrong with having an ego; we all have one of sorts. Each one of us includes inside our membrane a whole collection of things to which we are attached. By 'things' we do not mean simply material possessions, but literally anything: our abilities, expertise, opinions, skills, families, friends, sphere of influence, etc. In fact, any of the core values of the other drive states can be included within our ego membrane. For example, we can extend our ego membrane, or wrap our ego around our intellectual abilities – having a sharp mind can be a 'thing' that gives us self-esteem. It is what we include and exclude that gives us our sense of identity.

The Power drive is the drive that provides the energy and motivational force to extend ourselves. It is the drive to attach ourselves emotionally to 'things' which includes them within our ego membrane and affirms our identity. *We are often not aware of what we include in our ego membrane until we are threatened with having it taken away.*

 Self-awareness questions

What gives you your sense of identity?
Make a list of the things you consider to be 'me and mine'.
What loss would threaten you the most?
Use 3LT to explore your answers.

In our terms, developing a healthy ego means being able to expand the limits of our membrane to include more that we can identify as 'me'. We are aware that the act of becoming a more expanded 'me' can be perceived from some hilltops as a recipe for selfishness. However, it is far from a selfish act. We do it with our children and partners: we extend ourselves to include and care for them, we are concerned for them and we commit time and energy into helping them.

If we extend our ego membrane to include more people, more concerns, then it is far from selfishness, it is an act of love. Mothers die rescuing their children from a fire, people give their lives fighting for a cause and commit lifetimes to building a better society, because all have extended their sense of identity to emotionally attach themselves to some-'thing'. Selfishness is the opposite. Self-ishness is an unwillingness to extend our ego membrane to include and care for 'things' as if they were our own.

Having an ego is not therefore, as some might believe, a problem condition. Without one, it is difficult to imagine how we could care about ourselves, our families, what we do, etc.; without a sense of identity there would be nothing of importance in our lives. The problem is in the degree of willingness to include rather than exclude, to identify with more of the world rather than less. If our ego membrane could extend to include every 'thing' then there would be no separation of 'me' from everything else. (If you happen to have a Buddhist hilltop then you will recognise that it is the ego that prevents us from seeing our true nature. You probably will agree that the sooner we go beyond the illusion the better.)

The Power drive is the drive to extend ourselves, to confirm ourselves, to feel that we exist. It is stongly linked to self-definition. It is a powerful tool that nourishes our sense of identity and self-worth. Throughout this chapter we will be describing ways in which the Power drive manifests itself to build and develop this sense of identity.

The Power type

Power types are life's great energisers. Without the drive they bring little would get done. They are people of huge enthusiasm and energy, who thrive on making things happen. They are people who see life as a challenge and who measure success by what is *achieved*. Power types are the lifeblood of an organisation to the extent that they can become totally committed to what they do in a way that many other types do not. They are the people with the will to make happen what they want to happen.

The source of their energy and commitment is the inherently emotional world they live in. For a Power type, decisions are based not on rationality or logic, but on feelings, how things affect 'me', the pros and cons viewed 'from my position'.

Work

A career is usually the most important vehicle in life for satisfying the needs of a Power-driven person. Work has to provide challenge and the opportunity for success, be it in the form of financial reward, recognition, rapid career progression or a substantial sphere of influence. Work that attracts Power types is personal-performance related, dynamic and results-oriented.

Selling

The archetypal activity that draws Power types like a magnet is of course selling. We have yet to find an organisation where the sales force is not overwhelmingly made up of Power types.

Selling has all the ingredients that fulfil primary Power type values. What other career provides a better arena for challenge and success than the age-old art of influencing someone to buy something? In this perspective, selling is seen as a competition, both between the seller and the buyer, and between the seller and other salespeople with competing products or services. It is a situation where the Power type can put him or herself on the line and can legitimately use whatever power is at his or her disposal. Salespeople are encouraged to be assertive (and sometimes downright aggressive), self-assured and confident in themselves and their product. They are allowed to take risks, be courageous, persevere and not take 'no' for an answer.

 Self-awareness questions

Does your job demand selling?
What do you enjoy about it?
What do you dislike about it?
Use 3LT to explore your answers.

In the Jewish culture there is a word that describes the qualities of such a salesperson; it is someone who has 'Chutzpah'. Roughly translated this means 'having nerve'. Power types love the competition almost as much as the result (as long as the result is a win) and most sales departments acknowledge this need to compete: targets, quotas, commissions, internal league tables and Salesperson of the Year Awards are some of the established motivators for the Power type. They are all ways of measuring and recognising success.

Can you imagine the same accolades being granted to other roles – Strategic

Planner of the Year, Accountant of the Month, etc.? It is difficult to think of another organisational activity (with the exception perhaps of production) that is
so clear cut for the results-oriented: you make the sale or you don't, you get the
business or someone else does. Power types need something to aim at, clear objectives and clear measures of success, otherwise how do they know if they have
achieved anything? And what is also to the point, how does anyone else know?

There are some people whose contributions to a successful organisation are in
fact greater than any individual salesperson's, yet who actually prefer to remain
in the background. These are people who do not have the need for recognition,
and indeed would be totally embarrassed by it.

For Power types, however, recognition is of primary significance. It is of little
benefit to them to save the company from a major disaster or pull off a mighty
coup if no-one else knows about it. Not only doing the job, but being *seen* to do
the job is what counts.

Q. *'You have achieved all this in your career, you are successful, wealthy, you now
have a highly successful nightclub in London frequented by the rich and famous,
you are talking of America next. Tell me, what is it that drives you on?'*

A. *'Recognition, that's what it is. I love having my name in the papers, people
pointing at it, knowing what I have done.'*

From a TV interview with Peter Stringfellow

Status

It is difficult to convey how important recognition is to the status needs of a Power type, especially for those of you who cannot identify with it as a primary need
in yourself. Recognition by others is perhaps the greatest affirmation of self-
worth we can receive. Being seen as successful in what they do, or being perceived as powerful or influential, or being taken to be bigger, better, richer or
stronger – these are all sources of status for the Power type.

It is important to emphasise that almost all of us need recognition of some
sort. For some it is the recognition of being a good listener, for others it is of being knowledgeable or having an ordered mind. The Power type, however, needs
to be recognised for the qualities that are at the core of that hilltop, the qualities
of the Power drive.

Almost any activity can be a potential source of recognition for people with a
strong Power drive. The cars they choose are almost always top of the range,

their business clothes have the edge, their offices and desks usually bear the hall-marks of success. The way they deal with others makes people recognise them; the way they talk about themselves and their achievements sends out signals which demand recognition. Their willingness to declare strong opinions and assert themselves so that their point of view prevails makes them 'people to be reckoned with'.

 Self-awareness questions

What do you like to be recognised as?
How do you get recognition?
How important is recognition to you?
Use 3LT to explore your answers.

The difficulty many people have with the idea of personal recognition is one of self-aggrandisement. In order to exercise our Power drive, do we have to become selfish? The Power drive is by definition self-centred, being concerned with 'my' identity and sense of self-esteem. However, as we have described, *where* the ego membrane is drawn between what is experienced as 'me' or 'not me' determines the degree of selfishness.

The Power drive is not a selfish drive; therefore, it is the ego membrane that determines whether or not a person is selfish. In fact, being a value judgment, selfishness is determined inevitably by the eyes through which it is seen. We see other people's Power drive or the extent of their ego membrane, and it is we who, from our hilltops, decide whether or not it constitutes selfishness.

True, there are some Power types who are concerned only with themselves, yet there are many others who have an ego membrane extended to include the lives of countless others.

Power types can be inclusive and magnanimous. They can value themselves and can equally value others. They can include others succeeding in their success; they can be concerned for the welfare of their team, department, organisation or for the whole of society. Doing things that give them recognition often involves a whole group of people benefiting in many different ways.

In describing the qualities of this type, therefore, we have attempted to portray the energies of the Power drive in a way that includes both the selfish and magnanimous dimensions of the ego membrane without making a value judgment on either.

Self-awareness questions

What does selfishness mean to you?

How do you feel about people you consider to be selfish?

How selfish are you?

Management

Not all Power types are salespeople, although most salespeople are, as we have said, Power types. Many managers we deal with, across the broadest spectrum of business, are solidly of this drive and, predictably, it shines through in their management style.

Power type managers invariably lead from the front. They are the high energy, committed managers who expect everyone in their team to follow their example. They set high standards and high targets for their staff. The approach they take is very task-focused and results-oriented, e.g. 'I don't care how you do it or what it takes, I want it on my desk first thing in the morning'.

We recently worked with a project team in an organisation which had made great efforts to introduce a participative culture into its management style. The manager, a Power type, had really tried hard all morning to be facilitative and inclusive in her decision-making, drawing in the quieter members of the team, allowing lengthy discussions over minute details, etc. As closure was drawing near and a solution was still not in sight, she became noticeably more and more frustrated until she suddenly banged her pad on the desk and said: 'OK, that's it, this is what we are going to do'.

In three sentences, she then spelt out her solution to the problem and declared the meeting closed.

Power type managers can be fearsome entities, prepared to confront any issue or lack of effort head on. They are prepared to accept that they have a degree of power and responsibility and will be prepared to simply tell people categorically what to do when it is needed. They can, at the same time, inspire their staff with their own enthusiasm and drive, and will go to great lengths to support those they are committed to.

People often describe them as the best kind of manager: 'He demands a lot from us, stretches us, pushes us to do a first class job and won't put up with anything less, but he always backs us up. I've learned such a lot from working with him.'

Power types are self-starters and often very impulsive. Once they have made a decision they will simply go for it, whatever it takes. What may be lacking in a plan of action is often made up for by the energy with which they attack problems, simply burning through resistance or difficulties that would set others back. They are prepared to push, and bend the rules where necessary to get the result they want.

Power types are usually well-attuned to the politics within an organisation. It is highly relevant to the way they operate to know how the machinations of power work, who talks to whom, who needs what, what alliances need to be forged, etc. Consequently, they are very adroit at pulling strings and gathering the resources that they and their team need.

For many years we have been involved with the staff training centre of a substantial public sector organisation. A few years ago a traditional bureaucrat was replaced as head of the centre by a very dynamic Power type. A senior trainer commented, 'We have been pushing a heavy cart uphill for years trying to change things here. Suddenly it feels like we have to rein in a maverick horse to slow it down. Within the first morning she made ten major policy decisions.'

For Power types, making something happen successfully is a personal issue. They are emotionally attached to the outcome, no matter how large or small the issue, because for them, success or failure in the work they do reflects on their self-worth.

They are people for whom a half-hearted approach will not do; when they give, they give their all. They know the meaning of commitment. When they emotionally attach themselves to achieving something it becomes personal, and the challenge for them is whether they are big enough to manage it: They say, 'It's my baby and I am going to make it happen.'

Failure, therefore, is a far bigger issue for Power types than for most others. They have made a personal investment in success and facing failure means a potential loss of self-worth. Power types can take failure badly. Even if they are gracious in defeat they will often take it home and smart about it. However, for many, knowing that they did the best they could is enough: 'I gave it my best shot, so that's OK.'.

Self-awareness questions

How much does success mean to you in projects you undertake?
How often do you totally commit yourself to a course of action?
Use 3LT to explore your answers.

Power types are natural leaders – if only because they dislike being followers! They like management positions because, even if not at the top of the hierarchy, at least they have some sphere of influence: being in charge puts you more in control of your destiny than not being. We have found strong Power types in management in the Civil Service, one of the last places one might assume would attract them. These are the people who have the energy and commitment to carve out a sometimes quite substantial empire over which they have a considerable degree of control. There is nothing more frustrating to a Power type than feeling disempowered, having to get permission or to justify decisions before taking action. If a Power type finds him or herself in such a situation they will usually find another niche, or get out of the organisation quickly.

 Self-awareness questions

How much do you like to lead?
How strong is your need to be in control?
How much autonomy does your work provide?
Use 3LT to explore your answers.

Entrepreneurs

Of course, one of the places that attracts Power types is the world of the entrepreneur. Self-employment is the logical situation for those who want to be big fish, even if the pond is small. In the final analysis, being one's own boss is for many Power types the only employment that can satisfy their needs. It is the place where there is no-one to say 'no' (apart from the bank manager), where the risks you take are your own and it is down to you and you alone to make it work. And many do, through sheer guts, perseverance and opportunism. What was originally one person, a foot in the door of opportunity, a wing and a prayer, evolves over the years into an established business.

When we trace the history of most companies, no matter what size, we find that almost all started with one person with a manic drive to succeed and an opportunity to be seized. The Bill Gates, Rupert Murdochs and Steve Jobs of this world are examples of today's classic entrepreneurs.

Over the last few years, some of the larger organisations have been trying to reorganise many of their functions, decentralise and develop smaller business-focused profit centres. They have attempted to harness the entrepreneurial energy within the organisation by developing 'intrapreneurism'. They have recognised that for some types to be fully effective, responsibility must be matched by commensurate power.

 Self-awareness questions

How entrepreneurial do you feel you are?

Are you self-employed or have you ever considered self-employment?

If so, why? If not, why not?

Limitations

The undoubted strengths of Power types give rise, predictably, to a string of limitations.

Being forceful, energetic and assertive people, Power types make relatively poor listeners. When Power types want to make something happen, they can be very difficult people to argue with. They will put forward their opinions or proposals strongly and be prepared to handle whatever objections are thrown up. They can be guilty of cajoling, brow-beating, manipulation, stubbornness and any other emotion-based tactic that will produce a result. They can be insensitive to the needs, concerns and feelings of other people. Where they are invested with role power, they can become tyrants in the way they manage their staff: 'It's not whether you will jump when I say jump, it's how high'.

Similarly, having high levels of energy and commitment themselves, they expect the same from others around them and can be very intolerant and dismissive of those who do not come up to the mark. Rather than seeking to nurture and develop people, they often adopt a policy of hire and fire, simply getting rid of people whom they regard as a waste of time.

Power types' overwhelming need for action rather than words can lead to impatience and impulsive decision-making. They tend to work on a 'Ready, Shoot, Aim' approach; the idea of sitting down and doing some detailed planning or developing a strategic approach is quite alien to many of them. 'Get things moving, think on your feet, do a bit of nimble footwork to get out of trouble, but above all make it happen', tends to be their attitude to work.

> We were in a meeting with a senior manager and his second in command, a Power type. Eventually, the manager, aware of his second in command's obvious impatience and its potential effect on the discussions, leaned across to us and, with a pointed glance at his colleague, said in a jovial tone: 'You'll have to excuse him, he only opens his mouth to change feet'.

A Power type has no time to sit and thoughtfully digest a 40-page report meticulously detailed by a subordinate: what he or she wants is the bottom line, preferably on half a page of one sheet of paper. This often leads to poor planning and a lack of attention to detail (unless there is someone else around to do that kind of work). For those Power types who run their own businesses, the tasks that take a back seat are usually the paperwork activities: written quotes, cash flow projections, tight stock control, etc. Interestingly, these are the major reasons quoted for the high frequency of collapses of small businesses.

Power types can display other management weaknesses. Along with a lack of attention to detail comes the inability to brief staff in any real detail on a specific course of action.

Communications from the Power type manager tend to be more of a rallying of the troops or motivation session rather than a clearly spelt out battle plan. Such a situation is often compounded by unwillingness on the part of many Power types to delegate power or authority to others. Being largely solo performers, many believe that no-one can do the job as well as they can, and they are often quick to jump in and take control at the slightest indication that things are going wrong. This may eventually lead to disempowered staff being unwilling to take the initiative, and a manager who is confirmed in his or her belief that there is no-one to whom he or she can delegate.

 ## Self-awareness questions

How hard are you prepared to push to get what you want?

How impatient are you when preparation takes time?

How easily do you delegate power to others?

Leisure interests

For Power types, play is competition. In any game or activity their natural drive is to compete and win. It does not necessarily have to be intense and serious: in social situations there is the usual laughter and banter, but the excitement of the game and the challenge of competition is what really counts for this type.

In a TV documentary about cricket star Ian Botham, his wife, commenting on Ian's competitive instincts, described how he always plays to win. Even in board games with his child, she said, he cannot bear to lose.

When a Power type combines his or her competitive nature with the physical attributes of the Product drive, a competitive sportsperson may be the result. Whatever the sport, you will find Power types fighting for supremacy.

In some cultures, however, modesty in achievement has been the traditionally acceptable style. It has been acceptable to be a winner, but shouting about it has been frowned on.

Until comparatively recently, blowing one's own trumpet has been regarded as bad form, but this seems to be changing. Even in the most traditional of sports, it is acceptable to throw a clenched fist of success in the air.

Of course, even Power types cannot all be the best in the world: there are physical limits to their performance. They will, however, be constantly looking to be the best at whatever level they can, even if it is simply to win this particular game at this particular moment.

 Self-awareness questions

How much do you like to compete?
How important is winning to you?
Where do you get your challenges from?
Use 3LT to explore your answers.

Acquisition

Acquiring things is often a pursuit of the Power type. Acquiring the things that they value, and that are demonstrable signs of success, is a very important activity for many of these people.

Power types like to collect the unique or the valuable. Works of art, expensive jewellery, clothes from the most exclusive fashion houses, etc., are likely to attract their attention. Even if they never show them to others (which is rare), owning or wearing the symbols of wealth makes Power types feel successful.

At economic levels below that of the international elite, this drive can be seen in what Power types choose to surround themselves with. For many, the financial rewards of their work are put to use by acquiring things they value. What is it that makes people buy cars that cost as much as some homes, unless it is the status of owning them? Most of these cars are not an investment, as they depreciate enormously in the first years, and they certainly do not get through the rush hour any quicker than the average car. It therefore seems clear that the value for the Power type is more in the visible worth of such items, rather than in their intrinsic value.

 ## Self-awareness questions

How important are symbols of success to you?

What do you strive to acquire?

What are your most valued possessions?

Use 3LT to explore your answers.

If you are invited to a Power type's home for a social occasion, you might well find him or her the most generous of people. Power types share freely what is theirs, both in word and deed. But remember you are entering what is often the very core of what is considered 'me and mine' and it needs to be treated with the recognition that is expected.

 ## Self-awareness questions

Do you like showing off? If yes, what about?

Whom do you need to impress?

Use 3LT to explore your answers.

Security

Power types put their security in their ability to command and wield power. Money is the most obvious form of power in our society and the one that is used most frequently. Buying and selling, hiring and firing and wheeler-dealing are all based on the power of resources. Material possessions are a less liquid resource than money but are another expression of security.

Power types also place their security in their personal power. The power to influence events and people is, to them, the power to make things happen. Consequently, if you ask Power types who they value, it is likely to be the people who demonstrate these qualities: people who show real grit when the chips are down, the people who keep going no matter what, and are prepared to take what comes and give as good as they get.

 Self-awareness questions

What qualities do you value in people?

What Power qualities do you admire?

What are your Power qualities?

Negative aspects

We have described Power types as people with tremendous energy and commitment, emotion-based beings who thrive on competition and challenge. They are people for whom success in what they do and the recognition of their own worth are paramount. As we have said, many Power types fulfil their drives in an expansive, magnanimous way and are a joy to work with. However, when this drive finds negative expression it can be incredibly damaging, both to the individual and to other people around. Because of the strong emotional attachment to what they feel to be 'me and mine', Power types can very easily become possessive when they perceive a threat. Similarly, they can be extremely jealous of other people's success, particularly if it involves their own perceived failure. They can be resentful and bear grudges that turn into feelings of revenge: 'Don't worry, I'll get my own back'.

Because the Power drive is essentially about self-worth, failure often hits these people very hard. They may start to devalue themselves, sometimes with small comments, but at other times in the most severe of ways. They can become so committed to the perception of themselves as total failures that they can drop into a black hole of depression.

Another likely expression of this lack of self-worth in a Power type is to devalue everyone else around in an attempt to boost his or her own value. Rather than taking the basically positive position of life is a challenge, a Power type may see the world and everything and everyone in it as a potential threat to his or her personal survival.

Power types who adopt this as a life position become isolated within their own empires, trust no-one and are constantly looking for Machiavellian conspiracies which might usurp their power. The archetypal portrayal of such a stance is surely the character of JR Ewing in *Dallas*.

Negative Power types live in an egocentric world. They are absolutely selfish and completely committed to having their will prevail no matter what the consequences. From this position come the heights of coercion, manipulation and megalomania, where people are to be used and abused and where 'Absolute power corrupts absolutely'.

 ## Developing your Drives Profile – The Power Drive

What is your opinion of the Power drive?

How do you view the Power type?

How do you relate to people like this?

What does that say about your own hilltop?

Reflect on the answers you have given to the self-awareness questions asked throughout this chapter and make an intuitive assessment of how strong this drive is in you.

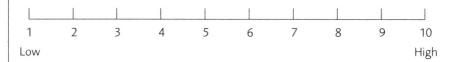

| 1 | 2 | 3 | 4 | 5 | 6 | 7 | 8 | 9 | 10 |
| Low | | | | | | | | | High |

Monitor your activities day by day and be aware of how much that you say, think and do is a readout of this particular drive. Be prepared to modify your assessment in the light of what you find and, later, in comparison with your other drives. For now consider:

How much of a Power-driven person am I?

How much Power drive does my work demand?

How much Power drive do I satisfy outside work?

Summary

The following are important to Power types:

Energy and commitment

Challenge and competition

Recognition and success

Influence and control

Acquisition and status

Those who are strongly Power-driven are good at:

Making things happen

Working as a solo performer

Getting their own way

Being totally committed

Taking risks

You will find Power types in:

Selling

Management roles

Dynamic situations, e.g. driving sales targets

Achieving results, leading entrepreneurial activities

Main work environments are:

Service

Retail

Financial services

Any sales-oriented sector

Small business

Outside work, people with strong Power drives are often attracted to:

Activity with a high competitive element

Winning and being successful

Fame and recognition

Acquiring things of value

Being well-connected

CHAPTER 9

The Plans Drive

Key traits: *Order, structure, logic, rationality, conceptualisation, organisation, authority, tradition, status quo.*

We have mentioned the idea of maps several times in this book. Maps are abstract representations of reality, attempts to develop concepts that we can use to describe and predict things in the world. The Plans drive is that part of the human mind that needs to develop concepts in order to understand experiences.

In the introduction to the Process drive, we discussed the idea of perception being part of the human information processing system, and Process types as those people who predominantly seek out new experiences to stimulate them. At the Plans level, perceptions are gathered together to form *abstractions* or *concepts*. There is a school of thought that believes it is impossible to have a perception without a concept. For example, without an abstract idea of a chair, do we see a chair or is it merely a construction of rods and boards with no obvious purpose?

When you see something that you have never seen before, do you try to describe it to others based on things that you know, e.g. 'It's a bit like…', or 'The nearest thing I can think of is….'

We carry masses of accumulated information, stored as concepts in the filing cabinets of our memories. These concepts allow us to use words and labels to order and understand the world, as we perceive it.

The Plans type

As with all the other drives, we all have the Plans drive within us. Without it, it would be impossible to read this book, for example, for words are the embodiment of concepts. Similarly, without the Plans drive, abstract thought would be impossible.

For people whose hilltop is predominantly shaped by the Plans drive, however, it is more than a natural ability: it becomes the central determinant of their world view and their behaviour.

For Plans types, the core drive is order. Above all else, these people have a need to order – and thereby make sense of – the world in which they live. Whether they are involved in elegant theories about the workings of the galaxies, or the sorting out of an organisation, a project or even a jigsaw puzzle, the central focus is one of making order out of chaos. If Power types are the lifeblood of an organisation, Plans types are the backbone and skeleton: they provide the structure of what would otherwise be mere jelly. Look at any organisation that lacks a solid Plans foundation and you will find chaos.

Work

The classic work situation for a Plans type is, of course, planning – in all its many forms. Plans provide order for organisational activity, a structure around which action should take place.

Most organisations (though by no means all) pay some attention to strategic planning. Some have whole departments full of conceptual thinkers, meticulously working out how to convert the company's mission into a two, five or even ten year plan.

Can you imagine the level of complexity, the mass of information and variables that need to be assimilated in order to plan with any accuracy how to move an organisation towards an agreed objective? It demands the ability to handle lots of abstract ideas and synthesising of projected future events into such a complex strategy.

Plans types are the people with those abilities. For many other types, the idea of spending weeks, months or even years wrestling with abstractions – with plans for an uncertain future – is inconceivable. (Even short-term planning for many is an irksome task. They use sayings like 'The best laid plans of mice and men' as justification for failing to plan.)

Plans types, on the other hand, have a great love for the workings and products of the mind. They actually enjoy planning as an activity, deriving great satisfaction from sitting down and developing a sound plan of action, whatever the scale of the project. The satisfaction for them is in being able to order things. Plans types are the people who enjoy planning their annual holiday meticulously: route maps, timetables, information on where to go and what to see, and an itinerary are some of the classic signs of a Plans type.

 Self-awareness questions

How much of your work involves planning?

What plans do you make for your future?

What do you like or dislike about doing it?

Another synonym of plans is the word 'blueprint'. A blueprint is an abstraction – of a building, for example. Buildings are planned with regard to other aspects of the Plans world – the laws of physics, the known properties of materials, building regulations, planning permission, etc. When people take an architect's vision (inspired or otherwise) and develop a blueprint, they are handling a set of abstract concepts with which to convert the vision into reality. This is predominantly the work of Plans types.

Without the attributes of the Plans drive – thoroughness and attention to detail, precision and accuracy in measurement and an ability to handle abstract formulae – we would have few wonderful structures, buildings, roads or machines. They are a tribute to the rigour of the Plans drive.

Science

Another huge area of work for the Plans type is science. Scientific methods basically combine the capacity to generate theoretical models (the Plans drive) with the ability to research, experiment and analyse (the Process drive). Hence we get both these types of logical thinking working together to hypothesise and disprove by experiment. In simple terms, they are exemplified by the professor, on the one hand, and the research student on the other. In reality, it is often the case that scientists have both the Plans and Process drives functioning within their individual make-up.

 Self-awareness questions

Does science attract you?

Do you find pleasure in piecing things together to understand them?

How important is it to you to understand how things work?

Use 3LT to explore your answers.

If scientific laws are the domain of the scientist, then society's rules are the domain of the law. We have a government and a legal system to make and apply rules to the way society and individuals within it conduct their affairs. The law is a vast area of depth and complexity, developed over centuries in an attempt to regulate and control human activity. It is society's expression of the Plans drive and attracts many Plans types to work within it. Throughout the legal system – from agencies and committees to courts, to law firms handling the vagaries of civil litigation or conveyancing of property – there are Plans types developing new legislation or using their knowledge of existing legislation, to conduct their affairs.

Law and order enforcement is a natural magnet for Plans types. They are people who will play by the rules, and seek to implement the rules in a fair, truthful and correct manner. Transgressions, such as police corruption or falsification of evidence, can come as a shattering blow to their deeply held beliefs.

The policy branches of organisations are often peopled by talented Plans types. A look at the policy document of your organisation will give you a good insight into the Plans drive. Administrative roles such as accounting, finance and budgetary control are often filled by Plans types.

 Self-awareness questions

Are you a rule-maker in your work?

What is your attitude to rules?

Do you administer procedures or policies?

Organising

Many Plans types who work within organisations do not fall into the specialist categories above. Whatever their role, a Plans type has a need – and usually the ability – to organise their work. In the main they are diligent and thorough workers who will pay the utmost attention to detail in the work they do. In many respects the Plans type is the traditional manager —someone who can be trusted to produce a competent piece of work, is reliable and shoulders the burden of responsibility willingly.

Unlike Power types, people with a predominant Plans drive have the ability to be dispassionate and rational in their decision-making. They are not like the experimental butterflies of the Process drive – they will take a project and sit down and organise things into some kind of order before making a decision on the way forward. Metaphorically speaking, they are people who use a ruler rather than drawing free-hand.

Limitations

Because of this overriding need for order and structure, one of the major limitations of the Plans type is that they can become rulebound. Some have the capacity to change the rules when they are outdated, restructure an approach to a task, etc. Others however, are happy to have rules given to them by those in authority and unquestioningly apply them – even when the situation demands a different response. This mentality can be summed up in phrases like 'Sorry, Sir, it's more than my job's worth' and 'Rules are rules, this is how we have always done things here'. The more codified a job is, the more there is a tendency for them to surrender autonomy to the rulebook.

Perhaps the greatest perceived limitation of Plans types is their apparent incapacity to take risks. From one perspective, their need for thoroughness, clarity and accuracy leads them to leave no stone unturned, no fact unconsidered in their search not just for a solution, but for the right solution to a particular problem. They can be very good 'right hand' people to provide the bullets that the Power type can then fire.

However, the same need for rigour often leaves them unwilling to take the risk of making the final decision. The deeper Plans types dig to develop a complete answer, the more they find they need to know. They can open up so many possible options, unknown variables, and potential risks, which all need further examination, that they render themselves unable to make a decision with any certainty.

Rather than 'Ready, Shoot, Aim', the philosophy of Plans types can be summarise as 'Ready, Aim, Check the target hasn't moved, Check the trigger mechanism, Plot the trajectory of the bullet, Ring for a weather forecast, etc.'

 Self-awareness questions

How willing are you to break the rules?

How thorough are you in preparation before taking action?

What do you need in order to take risks?

Use 3LT to explore your answers.

Status

Status for a Plans type is not attributed by power, influence, wealth or recognition by others. What gives a Plans type status is recognition by an authorizing body, whatever body that might be. In an organisation, status is bestowed in terms of rank within the formal order of the organisation.

A very clear example of this is the army. Another is the civil service, where there is a very clear grading system in which each grade brings its own symbols of status – a nameplate, a certain size of desk, one's own office etc: the organisation recognises an individual through his or her grade within the system.

Plans types love labels: they are the formal recognition of status within an organisation. Production Controller, Human Resource Manager, Supreme Commander in Chief, etc., are great labels for a Plans type to acquire. It is the investment of responsibility that is important, the formal authority that comes with the role that gives these people status. Sometimes a Plans type will accept a position that has a status label attached to it, even if it really involves a reduction in fulfilment, salary, etc.

The same principle applies to qualifications – academic, commercial or otherwise. To Plans types, formal accreditation is the mark of someone well qualified for the job. There are Plans types who invest a lot of energy in collecting qualifications to proudly display as badges to the world. And of course, there are many Plans types who look for these badges when looking to fit qualified people into positions within organisations.

 Self-awareness questions

How much status do you feel your role gives you?

How much importance do you attach to labels?

Which label or qualification would you like to have, and why?

Use 3LT to explore your answers.

Security

Plans types place their security in knowing where they stand in the order of things. When introduced into an organisation, a Plans type needs a clear and detailed job description. If Power types are those who are willing to get on with the game and blow the rules, Plans types are those who need to understand the rules before they feel comfortable playing.

The degree of their comfort or uncertainty is proportional to the degree of disorder and threat they experience. In a meeting, for example, Plans types are the ones who seek out clarity of objectives and will want to put some structure to the meeting in the form of an agenda.

Within several traditional organisations we have experienced the stress caused to many Plans types by being posted from heavily structured situations – where policies and procedures governed every aspect of their job – into other departments which demand a high degree of personal initiative. In many cases they have applied to return to their old department, or have attempted to turn a fluid, responsive approach into a structured, standardized procedure.

Plans types also place a lot of security in belief systems – conceptual structures that make their world understandable. There are many such systems around, which provide a coherent framework with which to comprehend the complexity in which we live. Science, for many, is not seen as a belief system but as a matter of fact, supported by hard evidence. The laws of science allow us to understand phenomena based on a set of rigorously tested guiding principles. There are consequently many people who believe that if something cannot be proven by such rigour, it is therefore invalid or simply does not exist. Yet there is a range of phenomena widely believed by others that falls beyond the scope of our scientific laws: fire-walking, UFOs, homeopathy, spoon bending, etc. For a Plans type, committed to a world view that holds to our rational scientific framework, these things are literally unbelievable.

The religions of the world are belief systems, adhered to by millions. Many claim their God as the only true God, so who is right? The Plans type is the one who will be able to develop what he or she considers to be rational arguments supporting a particular belief. The same is true of politics.

This whole question of belief systems and their relationship to the Plans drive is a difficult one. We all have belief systems; they are a fundamental part of our hilltop. What distinguishes Plans types is their need to be able to justify their belief in a rational and coherent manner.

> **?** **Self-awareness questions**
>
> What is the basis of your belief system?
> What do you dismiss as patently unbelievable?
> How fully can you articulate your belief system?
> Use 3LT to explore your answers.

What Plans types need, ultimately, is a framework into which everything fits and through which everything can be understood. Whether it is science, religion, law, politics or a homespun philosophy on life, there is great security for this type in having a set of guiding principles through which their experiences can be understood and their actions directed. 'There is nothing so practical as a good theory', goes the saying.

If there is security for Plans types knowing where they stand, one of the things that threatens them most is change. They are natural conservatives preferring stability to the disorder and impending chaos that change can represent.

There is therefore a great attachment to maintaining the status quo, in whatever situation they find themselves. Whether it is the introduction of new working practices, a dramatic reorganisation of the company or a change in the rules, you will find many Plans types resisting the change simply because it *is* change. To be acceptable to a Plans type, change needs to be thoroughly planned and undertaken very slowly so that it can be accommodated. Anarchy is the greatest possible instability for a Plans type.

 Self-awareness questions

Do you seek to bring change or stability to your work?

How much are you a creature of habit?

What was the last spontaneous change you made?

How did you feel about it?

Plans types tend not to be spontaneous creatures: to them, leaping before looking often leads to disaster and that in turn spoils the joy of leaping. They will want to study the map before setting off, read the instruction manual before switching on, etc. Their classic response to any new idea is usually: 'Hold on, let's just think about this for a moment'.

Leisure interests

There are many interests and activities outside the context of work that allow Plans types to fulfil their basic drives.

If it is sport, then above all, play must accord to some kind of rules. Plans types are the traditional good sports in as much as they will not flout the rules, will own up if the ball actually did cross the line and will accept the referee as the final arbiter in whom authority rests. They subscribe to the noble spirit of competition across the breadth of sporting activity: 'Play hard but play fair', and 'It is not the winning but the taking part that matters'.

Rugby Union has always been a major team sport for Plans types. More than any other international sport, its culture embodies the traditional values of the Plans type, according to the saying, 'Football is a game for gentlemen played by thugs, Rugby Union is a game for thugs played by gentlemen'.

Games of wit rather than will, whether physical or not, are the ones that interest Plans types. They find interest in games that require well-developed mental skills, strategic thinking and tactics as opposed to bluff, bluster or chance.

Bridge, chess and backgammon are examples. Chess particularly is a game where forward planning is the key to success, where the player mentally predicts the development of various options in order to decide the best possible course of action. It is also a game where knowledge can play a crucial role: at some levels of the game, players memorise classic openings, situations and even whole games, building up their repertoire of how certain positions have been dealt with in the past.

 ## Self-awareness questions

What games interest you the most?

What is it about them that is interesting?

What games bore you, and why?

Use 3LT to explore your answers.

Knowledge games attract Plans types. TV quiz programmes are wonderful showcases for people who have become expert in increasingly specialist subjects. There is tremendous satisfaction for Plans types in knowing everything there is to know about a subject.

Of course this drive is not confined only to games. Becoming an expert or an authority in a particular realm is something many do both in and out of work. When you hear being described as 'a leading authority on such and such', it is often a Plans type who has committed his or her life to studying, assimilating and understanding a particular aspect of the world.

If Plans types become collectors, they are noticeably different from the other types in how they collect. Whatever their collections, they tend to collect complete sets rather than one-off random items. They will strive to collect *all* the works of a particular author, or *all* the model cars of a certain period. Their stamp collections will be serialised, ordered and classified.

 ## Self-awareness questions

What do you collect?

Do you keep your collections in an ordered way? If so, why?

How strong is your need to put things in their correct place?

Use 3LT to explore your answers.

> **Q.** *'What do you enjoy about collecting stamps?'*
> **A.** *'I don't know, I just enjoy it as a hobby.'*
> **Q.** *'And what do you do with them, once you have them. Do you just leave them in a pile in a drawer?'*
> **A.** *'Oh no, I stick them into albums so that I can see which I still need to collect to fill in the gaps to complete the set.'*
>
> 38-year-old female

It was almost certainly a Plans type who first declared that 'One can only understand the present by understanding the past'. History is an interesting way of understanding why things are as they are, and lots of Plans types have an interest in an historical perspective. Whether it is political, natural, national, or local history, they are fascinated with understanding the development of the forces that shaped our modern world.

Combined with this is the interest in tradition and convention. If you look at our major Plans-driven institutions – government, religion, the legal system – they are marked by ritual and ceremony, sometimes dating back hundreds of years. One of their basic functions is to provide convention and stability: 'this is the prescribed way in which things get done; these are the rules by which the status quo is preserved'.

Following convention is one sure way of maintaining the status quo. Plans types enjoy understanding such rituals and the order in which things happen and why. The convention for discussion within Parliament for example is debate. Debate not only has rules of conduct, but combines another central love for Plans types – words. They enjoy vocabulary, the fine distinction in the meaning of words, and use it to weave logically consistent arguments in support of their particular positions.

If you have ever been involved in a group of people forming a club or society or simply holding a meeting, you will almost certainly have seen a Plans type in action. They will know the rules of the game, the conventions by which such things take place; they will understand the need for a constitution that sets the parameters of the activity, the rules that are needed to ensure democratic representation, election of officers, minutes of meetings, etc. A society's chairperson is usually a Plans type.

Both in and out of work, Plans types make wonderful committee people. Their natural style is to bring order to an activity – even a spontaneous game on the beach will be organised by them, picking teams fairly, marking out the court, clarifying the rules, etc.

 ## Self-awareness questions

How conventional are you?
How often do you find yourself in the role of organiser?
How would you describe your leadership style?
Use 3LT to explore your answers.

Negative aspects

When a Plans type's need for order and correctness is expressed in a negative form, it can become an extremely repressive force. The authoritarian stance, whether it occurs in the Victorian father figure, the rulebook manager or the die-hard right wing of Eastern European countries, serves to control and constrain individual freedom and liberty.

Plans types can become extreme disciplinarians, willing to enforce their beliefs, their particular version of the rulebook, with a rod of iron if necessary. It is not necessarily done out of malice: in the case of most strict parents, for instance, it is done out of love.

> *'I bring my children up by a strict moral code, that is, obeying the Ten Commandments. That includes being obedient and respectful to us, their parents.'*
> Seventh Day Adventist

When a Plans type has high levels of security tied up in a particular rulebook, a system of belief or any set of 'truths', he or she can become totally fixated and incapable of any change. The need for certainty can be so great that no degree of ambiguity can be tolerated. For a person so fixated, everything is black and white, there cannot be anything between.

Plans types can become so committed to maintaining a particular belief system that they will deny, reject and suppress any perspective that might challenge the basis of their beliefs.

In such cases, the very tenets of the Plans drive – logic and rationality – are abandoned and replaced by dogma.

Self-awareness questions

How willing are you to represent authority?

How strong a disciplinarian can you be?

What are the rules you live by?

What is your opinion of the Plans drive?

What does that say about your own hilltop?

 ## Developing your Drives Profile – The Plans Drive

What is your opinion of the Plans drive?

How do you view the Plans type?

How do you relate to people like this?

What does that say about your own hilltop?

Reflect on the answers you have given to the self-awareness questions asked throughout this chapter and make an intuitive assessment of how strong this drive is in you.

| 1 | 2 | 3 | 4 | 5 | 6 | 7 | 8 | 9 | 10 |

Low   High

Monitor your activities day by day and be aware of how much that you say, think and do is a readout of this particular drive. Be prepared to modify your assessment in the light of what you find and, later, in comparison with your other drives. For now consider:

How much of a Plans -driven person am I?

How much Plans drive does my work demand?

How much Plans drive do I satisfy outside work?

Summary

The following are important to Plans types:

    Order and structure

    Logic and rationality

    Conceptualisation and organisation

    Authority and tradition

    Security and maintenance of the status quo

Those who are strongly Plans-driven are good at:

    Working with abstract ideas

    Detail and precision

    Thoroughness and accuracy

    Organising systems

    Working within systems

At work you will find them:

    Developing and constructing theories and models

    In a planning capacity

    In administrative roles

    In organising situations e.g. as theorists, traditional managers,
    policy makers, leading committee members

All main industry sectors will have Plans types working within them.

Outside work, people with strong Plans drives are often attracted to:

    Activities that have clear rules

    Games involving mental skills

    Collecting for completeness

    Becoming an expert in a subject

    Maintaining tradition and convention

    Living by a set of guiding principles

CHAPTER 10

The Positioning Drive

Key traits: *Intuition, meaning, sensitivity, harmony, peace, integration, balance, intimacy, depth.*

The Positioning drive has until recent years been the most difficult drive to depict within the context of a business book – not because the drive itself is ambiguous, but because the predominant qualities of this drive do not sit easily within the typical organisation. Most organisations in our economy are essentially driven by Power or Plans and find little room for developing formal roles for the Positioning drive.

Nevertheless, there are many people who have Positioning as the major drive of their personal profile and it is therefore worth understanding the nature of this drive in detail.

The Positioning type

Above all else, what is important to people who have this as their predominant drive is a sense of *meaning*.

For life and work to be rewarding it has to be meaningful. Positioning types are not primarily interested in personal wealth or recognition, or the rapid career progression of the archetypal go-getter. They have to work for an organisation that is doing meaningful work, have a role that has meaning to them and develop relationships and lifestyles that are meaningful.

We use the term Positioning – a marketing term – to imply a sense of context, how things fit in relation to each other. Marketeers use it, for example, to describe the targeting of a particular socio-economic group with a specific product. The branding, image and advertising all position the product to fit the needs and aspirations of such a sector.

When we talk of Positioning types having the need to understand how things fit, we are not talking about the Plans types' need for building logical frameworks or orderly models built around conceptual abstractions. Positioning types understand things not through logic and hard fact, but rather through intuition and feeling.

What provides meaning for Positioning types is the quality of the relationship that exists between things, the 'how and why' rather than the 'what'. This is best illustrated by some examples.

Within human relationships, it is depth and intimacy that brings meaning. Positioning types do not seek the chirpy chatter of socialising that is the heart of People types' interaction, nor the intellectual cut and thrust of the Process type. For them, meaningful communication is found in sensitivity and the appreciation of others' worlds. The recognition that we all live in different worlds comes as no surprise to them, they are sometimes painfully aware of how separate we are as people.

In essence, it is this awareness that is behind their need to feel connected. Hence, when they build relationships with others, the connections come from the heart, not the head. They are people who rapidly gain trust through their ability and willingness to listen and share their more intimate thoughts and feelings with others.

The recent explosion in green issues is the most noticeable social expression of the rising awareness of the Positioning drive. This awareness has for many years been spearheaded by Positioning types: they are the people who are centrally concerned with humanity's relationship with its environment.

Central to the green cause are many of the key words associated with the Positioning drive: the fact that we are out of *balance* with nature, that mankind needs to live in *harmony* with the environment and to develop societies capable of *peaceful* co-existence and sustainability. Of course, not everyone who has become interested in environmental issues is a Positioning type: indeed for some it is nothing more than enlightened self-interest, or merely another trend to be played to as an advertising ploy. For Positioning types however, their concern is not for humanity *per se,* but for the greater interrelationship with 'Gaia', Mother Earth in all her complexity.

A further example of the drive for meaning and understanding that many Positioning types share is often expressed in their quest to experience a relationship with 'something greater than all of this', a spiritual force.

 ## Self-awareness questions

What gives meaning to your life?

What qualities do you seek in your relationships?

What environmental concerns do you have, and why?

Use 3LT to explore your answers.

Work

As already mentioned, there are very few formal roles within our typical organisations that are tailor-made to fulfil this drive. In fact we would suggest that few companies understand the nature of this drive and how important it is to company effectiveness. In the main, most organisational activity is anathema to the drives of the Positioning type.

Be honest – from this perspective, how much work that takes place within our organisations can be described as meaningful? When we look around our consumer-oriented society, how many organisations have meaningful outputs? How many organisations foster a culture of sensitivity and caring?

 Self-awareness questions

How meaningful is the work you do, and why?

How meaningful to you are your organisation's goals and products?

Does your organisation encourage sensitive communication?

Does it bother you whether it does or not?

However, there are niches – formal or otherwise – that Positiong types can occupy which utilise their abilities and satisfy their needs.

Market sensitivity

An ability that Positioning types often have is sensitivity to trends. When they read things or witness events, their natural tendency to look for meaning often leads them to see patterns developing from sometimes quite disparate pieces of information. Emerging trends are something that they feel intuitively, though they would often be unable to produce hard evidence to corroborate their early feelings. The Naisbitt Group, producers of *The Trends Report*, has developed a method called Content Analysis which scans thousands of sources of information each month to extract from them the emerging trends. For Positioning types, this is an example of the kind of hard evidence that would allow them to say, 'I thought so' rather than 'Gosh, I hadn't seen that coming'.

Consequently, Positioning types tend to be good at interpreting the results of market research. In fact, someone with a strong Positioning drive is more than likely to be able to point market research in the right direction. The boom in wholefoods and healthy eating was not born overnight, for example. In the Seventies, there was a tremendous upsurge in small local retailers (disparagingly described as the 'brown rice and sandals brigade' at the time). If any of the large food companies had spotted the trend then, they could have positioned themselves to dominate the market that has since emerged. Consider the recent rush for food producers and mainstream retail outlets to get health foods onto the shelves. Green political parties are also growing.

Companies which do not have Positioning types spotting emerging trends do not see opportunities until everyone else does – by which time it is usually too late.

Intuition, often called the sixth sense, is not something magical possessed by only a few. Do you recognise the phenomenon of having a glimpse of fore-knowledge about something, or perhaps a sense of impending doom? That is the product of your own Positioning drive at work. In scanning the environment with the focus on meaning rather than fact, usually below conscious awareness, we open ourselves up to the realm of intuition.

Exercise

Consider the following, and ask yourself 'What does all this mean for the future?'
- Many baby boomers around the world are the first generation for a long time not to have experienced war. They went through the liberal movement of the 1960s as teenagers and students.
- Many of our influential organisations are now being driven by that generation.
- There has been a tremendous upsurge in civil rights and protest groups in the last decades.
- The 'green' movement is becoming a major force in most industrialised societies.

If the Planning activities provide the skeletal structure of an organisation, then the Positioning activities (Marketing) provide its sensors. The buzzword is to be 'market-led'. We have 'the listening bank' and ad campaigns based on phrases like 'You watch while we listen' and 'Before we open our mouths we open our ears'. Unless organisations have good Positioning types in their marketing activities, in attempting to be market-led, they may find themselves a long way back in the procession.

If one ability of Positioning types is in spotting emerging trends, another marketing-related ability is image presentation. Because of the same sensitivity to the broader picture, these people are often intuitively aware of all the issues surrounding how a product might be perceived by certain groups. They can often be absolutely precise about the ways in which it should get presented to its potential market. Having a Positioning type as project leader can mean your campaign is conducted with foresight, sensitivity and appropriateness. If the person is a graphic designer or illustrator, those parts of the activity will capture the image well. Good Positioning types in this field can *convey* meaning as well as receive it.

 Self-awareness questions

What attention do you pay to trends?

Do you trust intuitive feelings?

How often do things take you by surprise?

Integration

Another area of interest for Positioning types is what we broadly define as integration. They often find themselves in an integrating capacity at work (even if it is one that is not formally recognised as such). Their need to work towards harmony drives them into positions where they become the *lubricant* with people, and between activities or departments.

To other people, Positioning types are often seen as natural counsellors. Their ability to forge strong trusting relationships means that people often come to them, sometimes with personal problems, sometimes to use them as a solid sounding board for ideas. They are perceived by others as genuine, concerned, and sometimes as sage-like. There are some directors we know who have a person of this type as their confidant or mentor. Whatever the issue or difficulty, people who use Positioning types as counsellors feel they have been listened to and leave feeling better thanks to the interaction.

Much of the essential activity that takes place within organisations is inherently disharmonious. There are predictable conflicts of interest between different departments over budgets, staffing levels, deadlines and a host of other issues. There are the usual hilltop differences that produce the 'them and us' mentality. The Positioning type's concern for integration can express itself at any level within the organisation and in any guise. He or she might be part of a management team looking at changing work patterns within their department, or a shop floor operative in a quality circle. Whatever the specific situation, the focus is a need to harmonise activities.

In meetings, these people will sit quietly reflecting on the wider context of what is being discussed rather than be energetically involved in arguing points of detail. They are often experienced as thoughtful and measured in their approach: 'Still waters run deep'.

When they speak, it is usually worth listening to because it often calls into perspective a more complete picture. The difficulty for these people in such situations is that the meaning of what they are saying is often not grasped because it is from a hilltop a long distance away from those who have their heads buried in content detail. And, not being the most assertive sorts of people, their valuable contributions can get lost or drowned in the clamour. Without the contribution of Positioning types, there is always the danger of a lack of foresight when developing plans. (For instance, there have been several notable examples of how a lack of foresight has led to major environmental problems.)

If the role of a Positioning type allows him or her access across different departments, you will often find him or her working in some capacity as a catalyst, helping to move the organisation forward by bringing things or people together in the right place and at the right time to allow a process to happen. It may be the classic manager who has been there many years – one who is not too organised perhaps but who knows the business; one who has, over many years, built a substantial network of solid personal relationships throughout the company. These are the people you will find popping in on other managers in distant departments, or having a quiet drink and a chat, suggesting small ways of nudging things on a bit.

Positioning types rarely want to run screaming down the corridors of power with their ideas, but work quietly around the edges, communicating with other concerned individuals to move things forward.

Sometimes you will find Positioning types with a formal role of change agent, working perhaps within an organisation development team. The focus on integration is often expressed by them developing the role of a facilitator or process manager, whereby new ideas come out of a process of communication between those charged with responsibility for implementation. The role of the Positioning type is to set up and manage the process by which this can be achieved, to draw out from the people involved their perspectives and ideas and work towards a point where they can all be synthesised into an agreed way forward.

As change agents, their concern for balance and harmony often leads them, at a macro level, to be concerned with the all pervasive nature of organisational culture. They are often drawn into working on initiatives that attempt to transform a company's culture. This might be improving communications, developing teams, increasing morale and commitment etc., but its aim will be to integrate the disparate energies and activities of the whole and producing a more positive working environment.

 Self-awareness questions

How concerned are you with integrating things?

Who uses you in a counselling capacity?

Are you a facilitator or an expert in the way you prefer to work?

Use 3LT to explore your answers.

We started this chapter with the idea that there are few formal roles within traditional organisations that demand the qualities of the Positioning drive. *We believe that one of the primary needs for organisations in the future will be to develop Positioning capability.* The rate of change is becoming such that companies need to refine their environmental sensors to read what is happening in their marketplaces and in society as a whole. They need to develop the capacity to scan the environment in a much more sensitive way if they are to spot emerging trends. They need to be open to a wide range of information, sensitising themselves particularly to fringe developments, for this is where trends usually show first.

They will also need to be much more in tune with the needs and aspirations of their employees and potential employees. Much of the success of organisations in the coming years will be in their ability to attract, retain and reward their people. The notion of reward is increasingly broadening from financial incentives to other ways in which organisations might seek to fulfil the needs of people who work within them. As you are aware, there are different fulfilments for different people. If you take the 7Ps as a way of profiling job satisfaction, for instance, there are many ways in which organisations can, and increasingly will, provide work and career paths that will gain commitment from their employees. The impact of these ideas on recruitment, selection and career development is enormous. It will be those companies which have actively developed the sensitivities of the Positioning drive that will be the ones most capable of response.

Limitations

Positioning types, like all the others, come in all shapes and sizes. At one end of the spectrum they can be solid individuals, committed to working in a balanced and harmonious way in whatever they do. At the other extreme, their need for harmony can render them ineffectual. They are not egocentric people and often find great difficulty asserting themselves. Because they value sensitive communication, the willingness to listen and empathise, they are rarely prepared to argue their case if it means standing up and forcing the issue. In fact, the thing that most Positioning types dislike is the ego energy of the Power types. To many of them it is this energy that lies at the root of many of society's problems: selfishness, acquisitiveness, the need to dominate, etc. This can lead them to be perceived by some other types as lacking strength when it comes to making things happen.

Another predictable limitation is a lack of pragmatism. While they undoubtedly care about the values they espouse, they may fail to realise the harsh realities of what needs to be done.

Success

To laugh often and much; to win the respect of intelligent people and the affection of children; to earn the appreciation of honest critics and endure the betrayal of false friends; to appreciate beauty; to find the best in others; to leave the world a bit better, whether by a healthy child, a garden patch or a redeemed social condition; to know even one life has breathed easier because you have lived. This is to have succeeded.

Ralph Waldo Emerson

Broader work

In their search for meaningful employment, many Positioning types find themselves attracted to careers or activities outside those that fulfil many other types. Some find employment in organisations that have within them an element of social responsibility – social welfare agencies or those with an educative role, for example. Others get involved with the meaningful activities of environmental agencies or conservation charities. Anita Roddick's *Body Shop* was a perfect example of an organisation that is founded on the beliefs that underpin the Positioning drive, and it caught the wave of green awareness wonderfully. As an organisation, its positioning was absolutely appropriate to the mood of the times.

Many Positioning types find themselves developing an interest or hobby into self-employment – not for the Power need to build an empire, but to create a lifestyle and a way of earning a living that has meaning. There are many who forego a career as such to find a healthy balance between working to live and living to work, who recognise that the important things in life are not found by achievement, wealth or success.

There are many Positioning types working as craftspeople, for example. Whether it is through weaving, pottery, textiles or whatever, they will be producing something that has aesthetic value and that matters, rather than presiding over a production line of meaningless knick-knacks for the tourist trade. In fact, for many, the balance between pursuing one's craft and earning a living through commercial production is a perpetual struggle: to produce a one-off thing of beauty is one thing, to make a hundred or a thousand repeats is quite another.

Art – in all its forms – can also satisfy the drive for meaningful work, particularly if it is conveying meaning in itself. We know a wildlife photographer who lives mostly in Alaska, working part of the year in the fisheries to support months of expeditions into the wilderness photographing whales, etc. He combines his pleasure in photography with a concern for wildlife and a need for adventure. His photographs are now being purchased commercially and are contributing to raising people's awareness of environmentalism around the world.

Restoration is attractive work for some Positioning types: restoring old furniture, machinery or buildings. It can be involved with the regeneration of our inner cities. That can include efforts to preserve archaeological sites that lie in the path of new roads, or returning so many acres or hectares of land to its original state to balance wetlands drained for the construction of new homes.

Over the last 30 or 40 years there has been a tremendous upsurge in the human potential movement. Born in the 1960s from a marriage of rebellious Process types and spiritual Positioning types, it has largely been avoided by mainstream organisations. Only the more conventional approaches to personal development seem to have taken solid root within most business communities. However there are thousands of developmental group leaders, lots of them with strong Positioning drives, running programmes in virtually every developmental activity you can imagine. Take any of the more esoteric magazines and you will find advertised a wide range of options from aromatherapy to guided meditation, psychotherapy, dance, the occult and philosophy. Positioning types are attracted to working in therapeutic situations, to liberating internal harmony as well as creating it externally with others.

 ## Self-awareness questions

Does the work you do involve beauty, aesthetic qualities, or creating better environments?

Do these things interest you as areas of work?

Use 3LT to explore your answers.

Leisure interests

Unfortunately, there are many Positioning types who find themselves in a career or a job that offers no fulfilment in this realm. So, how do these people typically satisfy their needs beyond the work environment?

To understand the activities that these people engage in we need to remember the key values: harmony and a sense of meaning. Leisure pursuits that satisfy this drive are those that fulfil these needs.

Communing with nature is an important one. There are few more essential activities for Positioning types after a week in a concrete jungle than to get out and recharge their spiritual batteries, and it may need to be far more than walking the dog.

Some go out to interact directly with nature, doing good work as a leisure pursuit. There are many deeply committed people involved, for example, in tree planting schemes, collecting seeds and raising them in nurseries for four or five years before replanting our dwindling stocks of indigenous woodland. The same is true for waterways, marshland and almost any area of ecological importance. There is a small but thriving industry that offers working holidays on organic farms, working the land and learning how to grow things without the use of modern fertilizers and pesticides.

 Self-awareness questions

Are you a nature lover?

What puts things in perspective for you?

What do you conserve?

Use 3LT to explore your answers.

It is hard to envisage a Positioning type that does not subscribe to the values of environmental organisations such as Greenpeace or Friends of the Earth. There are many who play their part in environmental campaigns at local level and on a voluntary basis by shaking donation cans in the street or collecting house to house.

While they are possibly top of the current agenda, it is not only green issues, however, that touch the beliefs of Positioning types. They are moved by man's inhumanity to man and by the gross stupidity of a world that puts political diplomacy above human suffering. They are concerned by things that produce violence, disharmony and imbalance in a world which could be so beautiful.

If the Earth were only a few feet in diameter, floating a few feet above a field somewhere, people would come from everywhere to marvel at it. People would walk around it, marvelling at its big pools of water, its little pools and the water flowing between the pools. People would marvel at the bumps on it, and the holes in it, and they would marvel at the very thin layer of gas surrounding it and the water suspended in the gas. The people would marvel at all the creatures walking around the surface of the ball, and at the creatures in the water.

The people would declare it precious because it was the only one, and they would protect it so that it would not be hurt. The ball would be the greatest wonder known, and people would come to behold it, to be healed, to gain knowledge, to know beauty and to wonder how it could be. People would love it, and defend it with their lives, because they would somehow know that their lives, their own roundness, could be nothing without it. If the Earth were only a few feet in diameter!

Author unknown

For Positioning types, harmony and the pursuit of meaning go hand in hand. They recognise that it is important to have harmony in the world and in their relationships, but also to seek harmony within themselves.

In the introduction to this chapter we briefly mentioned spirituality and religion. Many Positioning types feel uneasy about subscribing to a particular religion: Western religions particularly are rejected by many for the dogma and separation that they imply between man and nature. There are growing numbers who find the spiritual teachings of the East – Buddhism, Taoism, etc. – much more in tune with their essential beliefs in the 'interrelatedness' of all things.

Over the last few years there has been an upsurge of interest in the spiritual teachings of some of the American Indians. Their belief system places man in complete harmony with the natural world, a world in which all things command respect.

? ## Self-awareness questions

Are you interested in the deeper meanings of life?
What are your spiritual beliefs?
How important is a sense of inner harmony to you?
Use 3LT to explore your answers.

Another two important areas of this drive are 'esoterica' and culture. By esoterica we mean that huge area of interest that is not strictly spiritual or religious but is concerned with phenomena that lie outside of what is commonly accepted as scientific reality, things like clairvoyance, astral projection, psychokenesis, telepathy etc. There is an enormous body of cross-cultural knowledge going back thousands of years to support the belief that there is wisdom and awareness greater than many of us will acknowledge. Questions like racial memory, the ability of humans to communicate with animals, the influence of aroma on one's health and mood, crystal therapy, and other interests appeal to these drives. Positioning types may have greater sensitivity to these phenomena than others.

Regarding culture, works of great beauty – music, art, poetry or prose for example – are some of the most poignant expressions of meaning that can be found, and often have great appeal for Positioning types. They may or may not be accomplished in doing these things; the key is the appreciation of them. Also of interest to some Positioning types is ethnic appreciation – an interest in how different cultures around the world live, construct realities, establish systems of belief, etc.

Positioning types value deep personal relationships. Time spent with friends often takes the form of intimate contact. What is important to them within a relationship is honesty and sensitivity. These values mean that friendships for positioning types may take time to grow but will last a long time. They prefer the company of one or two sincere friends to a crowd of acquaintances and often do things together such as walking or simply sitting quietly together.

Faced with a People-driven social event for example, many of them would prefer to stay home with a book, go for a walk in the woods with a friend, or have a long chat on the phone or Internet. Unlike People types, they enjoy spending time on their own.

 Self-awareness questions

What forms of beauty do you appreciate?

What are your closest relationships?

What do you value about them?

Use 3LT to explore your answers.

Security

Positioning types put their security ultimately in faith. It may be faith in God or the universe, it may be faith in the essential goodness of life and human nature, or in the spiritual bonding with those they are closest to.

Positioning types, although they may well despair at what some see as the senseless violence and tragedies in our society, carry with them a faith that the inherent positiveness of life in all its forms will eventually prevail. However, such faith is not something that all Positioning types can maintain.

Negative aspects

One potential negative manifestation of this drive is a life stance not of faith but of total helplessness. Faced with the enormity of the universe, Positioning types can feel that we are nothing more than insignificant specks of transitory dust. From one perspective, recognising our place in the universal scheme of things is what is often referred to as enlightenment; from another, it can be utterly disempowering, a feeling that our brief existence has no *meaning*.

Do you find yourself, for example, feeling utterly helpless faced with pictures of mass starvation in Ethiopia? Positioning types who get into a negative life position can feel that way about everything, even the things that are potentially within their direct control.

Associated with this helplessness is a fear of the use and abuse of power. Positioning types at the best of times often find the whole notion of power difficult. It can lead them to become so scared about misuse of power that they refuse to use any form of personal power to affect their lives: they become victims of their own powerlessness. Sometimes it requires the intervention of friends or family to persuade them to stand up for their own rights, and those of others, no matter how terrible they feel about the abuse of power they may experience or witness.

Their fear of disharmony can lead some Positioning types to withdraw from the realities of the world and adopt a lifestyle that is driven by obsessive needs for peace and tranquillity. There are people who are so scared of terrorism, accidents or war, for example, that they will not be separated from their families for any length of time, in case an attack were to occur.

Some Positioning types feel the need for beauty and sensitivity so strongly that they become totally insensitive to other people's worlds around them. They might, for example, spend 20 minutes describing some inner experience of cosmic enlightenment that leaves you numb with boredom. Like all of us, when we get locked into our particular hilltop, they may find it difficult to recognise that, for others, their world may be totally uninteresting. But they will often shift gears quickly when this is pointed out to them in a light or sensitive way.

Developing your Drives Profile – The Positioning Drive

What is your opinion of the Positioning drive?

How do you view the Positioning type?

How do you relate to people like this?

What does that say about your own hilltop?

Reflect on the answers you have given to the self-awareness questions throughout this chapter and make an intuitive assessment of how strong this drive is in you.

1   2   3   4   5   6   7   8   9   10

Low   High

Monitor your activities day by day and be aware of how much of what you say, think and do is tied to this particular drive. Be prepared to modify your assessment in the light of what you find, and later, in comparison with your other drives. For now consider:

How much of a Positioning-driven person am I?

How much Positioning drive does my work demand?

How much Positioning drive do I satisfy outside work?

Summary

Positioning types regard the following as important:
- Meaning and sensitivity
- Integration
- Balance
- Harmony and peace
- Intimacy and depth
- Spirituality and faith

Those who are strongly Positioning-driven are good at:
- Being sensitive to trends
- Seeing the wider picture
- Integrating and harmonising activities
- Developing meaningful relationships
- Acting intuitively

You will find Positioning types:
- Working in market-awareness roles
- Working in counselling roles
- Working to integrate situations, e.g. enabling managers, facilitators, change agents
- Working to create something of meaning or beauty

Outside work, people with strong Positioning drives are often attracted to:
- Communing with nature
- Handicrafts and sensitive restoration
- Environmentalism in all its forms
- The pursuit of meaning through philosophy or spirituality
- Cultural expressions of meaning, beauty and aesthetic appreciation
- Developing deep, intimate relationships with a close few

Chapter 11
The Purpose Drive

Key traits: *Vision, mission, imagination, problem-solving, inspiration, enthusiasm, invention, originality, creativity, the creative process.*

If any level of our psyche can be described as being the most powerful in the effect it has on our individuality it is the level of Purpose. The Purpose drive is the expression of the core of our hilltop, an expression of the values and beliefs we hold about who we are and what we are striving for in our lives. In effect, our sense of Purpose dictates which drives we engage as our predominant ones, for example, if our purpose is to 'be somebody', the Power drive and all its qualities is the one which will predominate.

Our sense of Purpose can be seen as the *executor* of our individual drive profile. The focus of this book – understanding who we are and where we want to be – is essentially an attempt to discover our purpose and how we might fulfil it. For many people, the question 'What is my Purpose?' is one that is never asked. We choose our partners, decide on our career paths, make judgments and take action without conscious awareness of what we hold as the purpose of our lives. But, whether we are aware of it or not, we are all living out a purpose. It may not be a lifestyle that is presently fulfilling us, or a purpose that we are happy with, but everything we do is, at the deepest level, driven by purpose.

We are what we imagine ourselves to be – and our imagination is inextricably bound up with our sense of purpose. In this context, we are using the word 'imagination' to describe that part of ourselves that holds the images of what we believe to be true, the images we have about ourselves and the world we perceive.

In the Process chapter, we described how, as human beings, we take in information through our senses and discriminate between different events, feelings, etc. At the Plans level we develop maps – concepts that enable abstract thought, language, etc. At the Purpose level, the maps we develop and the *meaning* we abstract from them serve to create our beliefs and values and the images we hold that dictate how we judge things, our attitudes and our behaviour. (Some people simply call such a process conditioning. We prefer to think of it as a more dynamic interaction than the passivity that conditioning implies.)

Our life experience builds in our Purpose level, in our imagination – images that we then take for reality. These in turn dictate the attitudes and behaviour that are expressions of that particular point of view. Purpose types experience this process very distinctly.

We have all been brought up with a story. Some of it has been given to us, some parts we have reacted against and dismissed and some of it we have created for ourselves. Whatever the process, we have built into our deepest level images about who we are and what the world is and should be. Some people know from an early age what they are meant to do in their life – their sense of purpose is so strong that they seem to have little choice. For the rest of us, we often go through our lives following the path of our story without ever being aware of it. *The way we choose to live is an expression of our purpose.*

 ## Self-awareness questions

What story have you been told about you? (By others and yourself.)

What image do you have about who you are?

Can you write two lists? I am this . . . , I am not this . .

The imagination is a wonderful faculty. It can create possibilities where before there were none, or produce images that are so clear that the path by which they become reality is obvious. However, the imagination also has the power to imprison us by limiting what we believe is possible.

We can be limited by who we imagine ourselves to be and what we are capable of. We are not saying that anyone is capable of being anything he or she wants to be – clearly there are other limitations to consider. It is difficult, for example, to imagine a very short person becoming an international basketball star, though there are many examples of people transcending enormous difficulties to achieve their dreams.

 ## Self-awareness questions

What dreams do you carry of what you want to be?

What do you feel incapable of?

Why is that?

Use 3LT to explore your answers.

The Purpose drive

This drive is the expression of a person's sense of purpose. It manifests itself as a drive to fulfil a particular vision or mission which, for the individual concerned, is all-consuming. It is often a drive to create change, to take initiatives that develop something better: this might be a better product, a better way of doing things, a better solution or a better world. 'Better' in these terms means something that is more efficient, more elegant, more beautiful, less painful or wasteful.

The Purpose type

Purpose types are people who live in the world of the imagination. The images they create become the driving force of their lives as they seek to turn them into reality. *Their essential drive is to make real the things they imagine could be.*

It is difficult to generalise about where to find Purpose types – they occur sometimes in the most unlikely roles. They can be people with huge influence or, like most of us, never stand out from the crowd. The thread common to them all is a very clear sense of Purpose, a certainty about what they are trying to achieve. What separates them from other types is that what they want to achieve means breaking the bonds of the imagination, bringing into existence something that has not previously existed. In describing the qualities and behaviour of this type, we will start by looking at some of the biggest expressions of the Purpose drive – the people who have changed our world.

One expression of this drive is the visionary – the person who has a vision of a better future and sets out to achieve it. Mahatma Ghandi was such a man, Martin Luther King was another. They dedicated their lives to the fulfilment of a vision. 'I have a dream.' was not the cry of a wishful thinker but of a man determined to bring his vision into reality. Nelson Mandela is another good example of a Purpose type who has totally committed his life to achieving his purpose.

One person who changed substantially the face of the globe is Mikhail Gorbachev. In a few short years he set in motion energies that redrew the political map of Europe, and shook the cold war to its very roots. He is recognised by many national leaders as a man of vision.

Other Purpose types fulfil their life's mission in less global ways. Some, like Mother Teresa of Calcutta, are inspired by religious conviction to devote their lives to doing 'God's work' to help the suffering. Jackie Pullinger is a Christian missionary who has worked for 20 years among the drug addicts of Hong Kong's walled city – the place where she knew she had to be to fulfil her mission.

Of course, one does not have to be of this level of magnitude in order to qualify as a Purpose type: there are many visions to realise that do not demand changing the world, many ways in which the Purpose drive manifests that are a little closer to home.

 Self-awareness questions

Do you have a vision that you are working to fulfil?
How clear are you about what you are trying to achieve?
How inspired are you about future possibilities?

Work

One of the archetypal roles for a Purpose type is the Company Director – though very few directors we have met have this as their predominant drive. In this role, they are the ones ultimately charged with setting the company's goals and directing it towards its desired end. They are responsible for the encapsulation of the company's purpose, its Mission Statement.

We were once involved with the British part of a multinational machine tool company. For many years it had been a leader in its field, but the decline in the traditional steel industry meant that the company was facing a difficult future. The one Purpose type on the board was the Production Director: he was buzzing with images of where the company needed to go to develop new products, markets and services. At best, he was constantly met with blank looks, and at worst, dismissed as an irrelevance. The other directors simply could not move out of the prisons of their imagination to perceive any new possibilities. As the Production Director put it: 'They still hold on to the belief that we should be making machine tools.'

Much has been written in the last few years about the importance of a company's Mission Statement – how it should be the template against which organisational activities are judged. In *In Search of Excellence*, Tom Peters cites several examples of how the re-envisioning of a company's Purpose can liberate it into new marketplaces, how it can enable it to shake off the shackles of limited images that constrain it into being this and not that, rather than the possibility of being either or both.

Because of the difficulty we have mentioned in generalising about the situations in which Purpose types might be found, we will use the following as examples of Purpose types at work to describe the noticeable ways in which this drive shapes their behaviour.

Creating change

Working as managers, Purpose types are the ones who are driven to create change. Whereas a typical Plans type will want to administer a steady environment, the Purpose type is the one always searching for how to make things better. Purpose types are often characterised by their undying enthusiasm: in the pursuit of their goals they can often become quite obsessive, even manic. If you happen to work with one of these people, notice how they champion their cause, how they take every opportunity to advance it, share the vision, and inspire others with their enthusiasm for the change they are pursuing.

Purpose types can work with long time horizons. Change is an ongoing process, and some changes by their very nature take a long time. It may be incomprehensible to other types that these people can work towards an image that may be five or ten years ahead. Again, it is the clarity of their vision of the future that makes present day activity purposeful to them. When a vision is held so clearly, here-and-now decisions are easy, the basic question being always 'Is it in line with the vision, or is it a diversion?'

 Self-awareness questions

How strong is your drive to create change?

How enthusiastic and committed are you in your work?

How far into the future does your vision extend?

Use 3LT to explore your answers.

Developing images takes effort. It takes a willingness to play with possibilities, to suspend the tendency to dismiss things as impossible, to open up the imagination to new perspectives. It demands a close examination and constant updating of the maps we hold, and an understanding of how these can limit what is possible by being taken as inviolate and therefore never being questioned.

For Purpose types, an image of what they want to achieve is much more than a goal. If a goal is represented by a straight line, then an image is a complex three-dimensional spider's web. Consequently, these people often work in a multi-dimensional way, seeking to achieve many different goals simultaneously. They are always creating new goals to achieve, looking for new problems to solve that are in line with their overriding purpose.

When Purpose types communicate with others, it often feels like inspiration. Through their enthusiasm they have the ability to leave others feeling excited by the possibilities they are opening up. They tell people about their mission, enthuse, and discuss problems and solutions. They ask others about what they are trying to achieve, constantly getting excited by new ideas and opportunities.

One very noticeable trait of Purpose types is their use of language. They convey images through the use of analogies and symbols rather than fact or detail. They have the ability to paint pictures in the imagination, images that set other people's imagination alight. The visionaries we referred to earlier all used the language of the imagination. Ghandi's marching to the sea to gather salt and his use of the spinning wheel were both symbolic representations of his message. In practice, anyone who shows leadership by painting attractive visions of what is possible is exercising the same Purpose drive, whatever their field.

 Self-awareness questions

Who do you feel inspired by?
Do others ever feel inspired by what you do?
Do you understand the power of visionary language?

Science

Modern society has developed along its technological path largely because of the work of a small number of visionaries in the field of science. Imagine, for example, a world without electricity. Nikola Tesla was the first man to discover alternating current electricity and to unleash its power, the first man to tap the hydro-electric power of the Niagara Falls with his turbines. His biography describes how he could build a machine from its constituent parts, view it from any angle, run it for a hundred hours and measure the wear on it – all in his imagination!

Nearly all scientific breakthroughs have been made by Purpose-driven people. Newton had been pursuing scientific disciplines for many years when the famous apple dropped on his head. His breakthrough was the result of many years of purposeful activity in his field. When people commit their lives to the mission of scientific discovery, they live on the outer edges of possibility. For example, theoretical physicist Professor Stephen Hawking sees his mission in life as postulating ideas about the nature of the universe. His work has included the theory of black holes in space, where the mass of something the size of the Sun has imploded to the size of a football and where gravitational forces are so strong that not even light can escape. Since he first put forward this idea several years ago, evidence has emerged to back up his theory.

Bright Purpose types are always in demand in research and development. In disciplines from civil engineering to computer technologies, their creative vision, their thirst to solve problems and to break new ground, leads them to significant technological breakthroughs. *Remember that every man-made thing, however small, started in someone's imagination.* Watches, calculators, telephones, etc. are all products of someone's imagination.

'Creatives'

The common thread that links Art and Science is creativity: both involve working with the imagination to create something that has not previously existed, something that is original. Purpose types find expression for their creativity in a wide range of activities.

Firstly, there is pure art, and the undisputed genius of the world's great artists. Throughout history, Purpose types have unleashed their creativity in the form of painting, sculpture, music, writing, film etc. For many, the medium seemed to matter little – they were all available vehicles for creative output.

There is also what might loosely be defined as applied art – the whole field of design. Whether it is architectural, landscape, interior, fashion or any other design activity, it is a creative process dealing with images, form, textures, materials etc. There are lots of creative Purpose types in advertising today, bringing innovation and originality into media presentations. They find their forte in 'think tank' situations where they often provide the seed of inspiration for a new image. For some, being surrounded by other creative individuals willing to play with and extend new ideas is the best possible environment. Their energy and enthusiasm leads to streams of creative ideas, which then need channelling and harnessing to be of value to the industry.

 Self-awareness questions

How creative are you in what you do?
What new ideas have you initiated recently?
How much room for creativity is there in what you do?
Use 3LT to explore your answers.

Status

Ultimately, Purpose types get a sense of status from acclaim: not necessarily the acclaim that many Power types seek of being famous or publicly recognised, but of acknowledgment by their peer group. Being respected by people they respect for their genius or creativity is, to a Purpose type, the only true mark of status, for it is acknowledgment by the few people who really know something about the subject. Being a writer's writer, or being invited to exchange ideas freely within an elite scientific community, means being valued as a creative individual, an equal among equals.

Limitations

History is littered with the stories of Purpose types who ended up as paupers. Why is it that many of our most creative talents do not enjoy material prosperity as the fruit of their labour?

When so much importance is placed on creativity, and when a Purpose type has his or her head full of fantastic images bursting to get out, worries about mundane things such as money or whether their work will sell can become irrelevancies. To this day, patrons still save some such people from having to deal with the distractions of day-to-day existence. Many others, however, are not so fortunate and spend their lives in poverty. Though few would ever contemplate giving up their purpose, their impoverishment means that they often cannot buy the things necessary for the free expression of their creativity.

The inherent limitation with Purpose types is that it takes more than the imagination to produce results. The creative process has to start with an image or vision, but there are many other qualities needed to develop the vision into something real and tangible.

A major reason for failure among such types is narrowness of focus, an unwillingness or inability to follow creative ideas through to embodiment in a product. They have other ideas to get on with, lots more creative ideas they need to explore. It is often the same with solutions to problems. Once a problem has been cracked, some Purpose types simply lose interest in the implementation of their solution as they turn their attention to what is important to them, i.e. more exciting problems to solve.

A Purpose type can be extremely valuable to an organisation. If there are others around to pick up the ball and run with it, if he or she combines energies with a Power type for example, both can be successful in their own terms. If, however, the Purpose type has to do it all, the vision may falter at some stage of the process and never reach the world as tangible output, remaining just another great idea that fails to see its fullest unfolding or implementation. The limitation that many Purpose types have, therefore, is their incapacity to translate their vision into action.

Self-awareness questions

What do you sacrifice to fulfil your purpose?
How often do your ideas get left on the shelf?
How important as an activity is solving problems?

Leisure interests

If work is a major outlet for the drives of a Purpose type, they are likely to spend their leisure time engaged in totally opposite kinds of activities – drinking, socialising, sport, etc. If a Purpose type does not have work as an outlet for his or her creativity, however, it can be expressed in several ways outside work.

For people who predominate at the Purpose level, the distinction between work and play can become quite blurred. In both, they are absorbed with the magic of the imagination. They will spend hours toying with new ideas or inspiring images in a carefree and often childlike manner.

The classic image of the Purpose type at play is the crackpot inventor: the person who by day has a regular job, but who by night has his or her own private mission to fulfil. They are still around, coming to public attention occasionally in the press or winning awards for wonderfully simple yet ingenious ideas.

A colleague of ours is a good example of a Purpose type. For many years he has worked in a regular job at a reasonably senior level. He has a passion for education, particularly for developing ways in which learning can be accelerated. His spare time is devoted to creating games which enable complex ideas to be quickly grasped. He turns up at our meetings with a case full of prototypes in various stages of completion, and a mind whirling with ideas. He has recently approached some of the larger game manufacturers with his ideas and is having some success.

Purpose types love solving problems – not the kind to be found in brain teaser books, but problems that as yet have no known solution.

Some people find outlets for their Purpose drive in leisure by absorbing themselves in the arts as creative activities. They may paint, draw, sculpt, work in wood, clay, metal, etc., or work with words, music or their bodies as mediums through which they can express themselves. There is an almost endless variety of activities for the expression of creativity.

Some find fulfilment in absorbing themselves in the creativity of others. They appreciate the creative process in many forms, going to the theatre or cinema, studying art and literature. They get inspired not only by the products of the imagination but by reading biographies about the lives of other creative people.

Of course many Purpose types have no public claim to fame whatsoever; they simply devote their life outside work to the pursuit of their dream. There are people, for instance, who have found a burning desire to change their lives, and who commit themselves wholeheartedly to changing their situation. There are those who have endured a great deal of hardship to turn themselves from a nurse into an actress, a bank manager into a singer, a carpenter into a wildlife photographer etc.

When people become in touch with what they really want to do in life, they are in fact turning on their Purpose drive. They can become totally inspired and dedicated to the pursuit of their goals; nothing else matters except fulfilling the image of who and where they want to be. In the following chapters we will look at how strong *your* desire to change is, and how to go about it.

 Self-awareness questions

What creative interests do you pursue?
Do you have an overwhelming mission?
Are you working towards changing your life?
Use 3LT to explore your answers.

Negative aspects

The line between genius and insanity can be a fine one. In its negative expression, the Purpose drive can literally be what is perceived as insanity. Living in the imagination as Purpose types do, it is, relatively speaking, less of a leap into insanity than for others who are more grounded in everyday reality. Many famous Purpose types have histories of mental illness, manic depression etc. If not actually regarded as mad, many of these people were, at the very least, a bit eccentric. When visions do not become realities, they remain fantasies – and living in a world of fantasy is a readout of a Purpose drive that is unable to find expression.

Another negative aspect of this drive can occur in the vision that is being carried. Visions are very powerful things, and visionaries can be very charismatic people. Most of us would subscribe to the positive visions of Ghandi and Martin Luther King for example, but in his own way Adolf Hitler was also a visionary. He certainly had a very clear mission, he inspired millions of people with his vision and charisma, and yet his vision, certainly by most people's values, was a negative one. Negative visions can inspire people to do horrendous things, just as positive ones can inspire the opposite.

At this level, we are subjected to a war of visions: capitalism versus communism, religion versus politics, and environmental protection versus unsustainable growth. Every one of us needs to know what visions we hold about our purpose; otherwise the danger is that we get a vision dropped on us by others. Whether the vision is global or local, we need our own yardstick to measure it.

Developing your Drives Profile – The Purpose Drive

What is your opinion of the Purpose drive?

How do you view the Purpose type?

How do you relate to people like this?

What does that say about your own hilltop?

Reflect on the answers you have given to the self-awareness questions throughout this chapter and make an intuitive assessment of how strong this drive is in you.

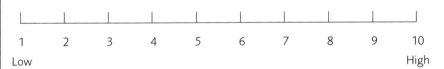

| 1 | 2 | 3 | 4 | 5 | 6 | 7 | 8 | 9 | 10 |

Low   High

Monitor your activities day by day and be aware of how much of what you say, think and do is a readout of this particular drive. Be prepared to modify your assessment in the light of what you find and, later, in comparison with your other drives. For now consider:

How much of a Purpose-driven person am I?

How much Purpose drive does my work demand?

How much Purpose drive do I satisfy outside work?

Summary

The following are important to a Purpose-driven person:

Vision and mission

Imagination and problem-solving

Inspiration and enthusiasm

Invention and originality

Creativity and the creative process

Those who are strongly Purpose-driven are good at:

Developing and championing visions

Using imagination to solve problems

Working with total commitment and enthusiasm

Making creative breakthroughs

You will find Purpose types:

Working in an envisioning role

Working to create positive change

Working as 'creatives', e.g. scientists, innovators, designers, artists

Outside work, people with strong Purpose drives are often attracted to:

Activities that stimulate the imagination

Inventing and discovering things

Artistic ways of expressing images

Working towards achieving a purposeful goal

PART 3 WORKING TOWARD CHANGE

CHAPTER 12

Developing Your Unique Drives Profile

In describing the seven very different drive states, we have focused on the idea that when a particular drive predominates within an individual's hilltop, it gives rise to certain predictable qualities and characteristics. It determines what is important and valued, what perspective the individual takes, and how he or she typically will strive to satisfy that drive.

We have developed a typology based on the 7Ps of drive around this notion of predominance, describing a particular type as someone who operates predominantly from one of the drive states to the exclusion of most of the others. In our experience, such people do exist. There is a very distinct quality to almost everything they say or do. They broadcast their 'type' message loud and clear – almost as though they had already read this book and are faithfully playing the part! We hope that in reading the previous chapters you will have recognised people you know or deal with who are clearly distinctive as a type.

The messages that others broadcast are not so obvious. It takes a degree of sensitivity to hear what messages are being given out, and often we need to ask the deeper questions in the Three Level Technique (3LT) to make the distinction between a person's behaviour and their motivation. If we do not take the time to develop these skills, then our understanding both of ourselves and others can be based on flimsy data and gross assumption.

The purpose of introducing types is not to enable you to categorise and put people in boxes, it is to enable you to recognise the distinct qualities and characteristics that arise from each *drive state*. Most of us are driven by combinations of drives, in differing strengths and relations to each other. If we are to understand something of our innate complexity, we need to know how these drives interrelate in producing our own unique hilltop.

In Chapter 3 we introduced the possibility of seeing these drives operating in a dynamic state, represented by a drives profile, with individuals being able to understand the relative dominance of the different drives in their own make-up. Throughout the 7P drive chapters we have posed a series of questions to heighten your awareness of your identification with each drive. If you have taken the time to reflect on them, you will by now have a fairly clear picture of your relationship to each.

In this chapter we want you to take stock of your findings and draw them together to build your personal drives profile. From there you will be in a position to make choices about how you want to fulfil your drives, and what changes you may wish to make.

Building your drives profile

At the end of each drive chapter, we asked you to make a subjective judgment about the strength of that particular drive in your hilltop and to score it from one to ten. Since then you may have had time to monitor your motivations and behaviour and may wish to amend your score. We need to stress that this is *your* assessment, and later we will discuss ways of confirming or refining your judgment.

For now, however, simply translate your scores from the individual chapters onto the following collective drives profile to build a bar graph.

Personal Drives Profile

Self-awareness questions

Which are your more dominant drives?

What does that mean to you?

In the light of this comparison, do you need to reconsider any scores?

A work drives profile

If the above exercise is your self-assessment of the different drives you have, we can also subject your work to the same process to gain a degree of comparison between what your dominant needs are and which drives are *demanded* and *satisfied* by the work you do. Throughout the 7P drive chapters we have asked questions about the work you do. Reflect on your work in terms of how much it demands that you operate in the different drive states, e.g. 'How much does my work demand that I engage my Power drive?'

Work Drives Profile

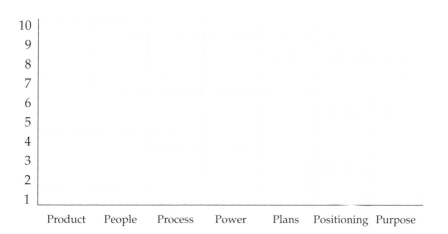

 Self-awareness questions

What correlations are there between your personal and work drives profiles?

Which drives do you satisfy at work?

Which drives do you not?

Which drives does your work demand more of than you feel you have?

Outside your work environment – leisure interests

The third drives profile we need to create is about the drives you seek to satisfy in your interests and activities outside your work environment. Reflect on your answers throughout these chapters and plot a drives profile of which drives you predominantly engage outside work.

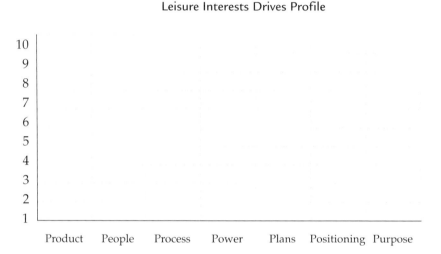

Leisure Interests Drives Profile

? Self-awareness questions

Which drives do you predominantly satisfy outside work?

Which of these do you engage in as an attempt to balance the lack of fulfilment of them in work?

Do you see any drives that are satisfied both in and out of work?

Do you have any drives that have no means of fulfilment at the present time?

In comparing these drives profiles, what meaning have you taken from them? *Are you in a job, a role, or a career that is fulfilling your needs? Does your work demand that you have to engage a drive or drives that you prefer not to? Are there changes you would like to make, or is the total balance something that you are happy with?*

There may be changes you would like to bring about, and the next chapter offers some thoughts and possibilities for tackling change. Before that, however, we need to address the important issue of developing sensitivity. Without it, changes may not happen as we wish.

Developing sensitivity

We have introduced you to the 7Ps of personal drive as a way of mapping and understanding some of the fundamental forces that shape your unique hilltop. We have introduced the Three Level Technique (3LT) as a means of exploring some of the depth behind why you do what you do. However, it has only been an introduction, a first pass over a very complex area. We have only covered some of the more prominent features of each drive; the subtleties and richness of behaviour that each drive results in are immense. Like any map, the more you study it, the more detail you will find.

Unfortunately, we know of no way to achieve a clear, objective measure of who we are. Even if it were possible to compute brainwave activity of the different drives and produce a high-tech printout of our drives profile, that information would have to go through our subjective processing system to be made sense of, accepted or rejected, distorted or suppressed.

So the questions is, how can we develop enough sensitivity to the predilections and biases of our own hilltop to be able to see ourselves and others with any degree of clarity? How can we compensate for our natural tendency to perceive things in a certain light?

Taking responsibility

Firstly, and most importantly, we need to be able to take responsibility for our own perceptions. Without doing this, we can never begin to give ourselves choices about how we perceive ourselves or others. By taking responsibility, we mean *recognising that the way we see things is only the way we see things, and not necessarily objective fact.* It is all too easy, particularly where other people are concerned, to forget that we are interpreting them or their behaviour.

 Exercise

Think of someone you find very difficult to like – maybe someone you know personally or a public figure – then complete this sentence: 'I find it difficult to like them because they are too....'

Our reasons for disliking people are inexhaustible – there are so many quirks and qualities that make others unendearing. Yet unendearing to whom? Presumably the people you find it difficult to like have friends or colleagues who do not share your perceptions.

So, when someone is too this or that, who is doing the measuring, and by what standards? There is no objective yardstick for any of our reasons for disliking someone. It is a totally subjective measure based on how far away from our own hilltop those people are. If we value assertiveness, then people can easily be seen as too soft; if we value flexibility, they can appear too dogmatic, and so on. Yet people may not be too this or too that – this is only our judgment of them from where we stand.

 Self-awareness questions

Take the sentence you completed in the previous exercise.

Do a 3LT analysis on it – ask yourself:

What is it about that characteristic that I find difficult to take?

What does that say about me as a person?

To take responsibility for how we perceive others, we need to recognise that our judgment of other people is based not on indisputable observation, but on the filters of our value system.

Observing the observer

We are, of course, back into values, importance and drives. *What we like or dislike in a person often says more about us than about that person.* We, the observers, are making judgments based on what we value.

At the end of each drive chapter we asked you how you viewed each drive, how you related to this type of person. Your reaction to the qualities and characteristics of each drive can give you insights into your own drive states. If you take responsibility for how you perceive others, your reactions to them can teach you a lot about the relationship between the different drives that operate within you.

What we see in others is a mirror of ourselves. We are not suggesting a direct mirror image: for example, if you see someone as ruthless it does not necessarily mean that you are ruthless too. When we describe others as a mirror, we mean that you can use your reactions to them to reflect on yourself. You can become aware of the part your hilltop plays as the observer by asking yourself what your views of others are telling you about yourself.

We have found that there are some predictable interactions between the different drives, predictable ways in which one type will see another. Plans-driven types, for instance, tend to value logical thinkers, People-driven types value concern for others. If we do not operate from the Power drive, we will tend to see those who do as selfish, those who operate from the Product drive as gross, etc. The possible combinations are endless. We can see drives as positive or negative. We can appreciate a drive in others that we feel lacking in ourselves, or have a drive within us that we dislike or reject when we sense it in other people.

The point is that whatever we see, we can use it to learn about ourselves. If you find yourself reacting to anything, examine your reaction. Ask yourself what it is that you are reacting to. Be prepared to do a 3LT analysis on your reaction. If you like or dislike something, try to understand the basis of your response rather than simply accepting it as likeable or not.

The role of feedback

Of course, even with a mirror, we cannot see the backs of our own heads. Neither can we tell how accurately we interpret the reflections. Another way of sensitising ourselves to our own predominances is to get feedback from others.

Of course, we get feedback from others all the time, and we are not suggesting that you listen to all of it. You accidentally cause someone to spill their drink and for the moment you're a 'clumsy idiot'. You forget an appointment and you're 'totally disorganised'. There is feedback and there is feedback, and it can be difficult to separate out what is real and valuable from what is simply other people's projections onto you. When someone gives you feedback, they are subject to their own hilltop colouration just as you are to yours. Out of the richness of your personality, people will tend to pick out things that are important to them, things that they like or dislike.

Having said all that, feedback is crucially important if we are to be able to check out our perceptions of who we are. If there is a gap between how we perceive ourselves and how others perceive us, it can create a great deal of confusion. Without reliable sources of feedback it is possible to delude ourselves and live in an internal reality that does not match up to other people's experiences and perceptions of us.

During a recent counselling session, a colleague of ours mentioned how angry she frequently got – with her children, in her work, etc. The rest of us were surprised by this as her demeanour was always one of calmness and staying in control. We told her that we had never seen her get angry, and that if she did, then she had not expressed it in our presence. Her internal image of being a person who felt and expressed anger was not matched by our feedback. The feedback helped her correct her image of herself.

The question is how can we get feedback of the right quality and what can we do with it once we have it? There are no hard and fast rules, but here are some tips that might help:

1. You must want feedback. You must actively seek it out and be open to listening to it. Unsolicited feedback is of dubious value and often more for the benefit of the giver than the receiver.
2. There must be a degree of trust. The giver must have some credibility in your eyes for you to listen to their views about you.
3. Feedback needs to be as near to objective observation as possible, rather than being condemning judgment. If there is a judgment being made by the giver, he or she is clouding the feedback with personal values.
4. Feedback must be specific. Asking 'What do you think of me?' does not help you a great deal, except to show what qualities the *giver* looks for in people. You need to ask specifically about areas that you want feedback on, e.g. 'How assertive do you experience me to be?' You can ask about all the different drive states by using appropriate questions.
5. Be prepared to explore the answers you get, and ask for examples, situations or incidents of how you behave and what effect it has.
6. Listen to the feedback! This may appear to be stating the obvious, but there are many reasons why we close our ears. The most difficult kind of feedback for some of us to accept is supportive feedback, the sort that confirms the positive aspects of our character. For others, corrective feedback – which gives us the opportunity to modify our behaviour – can all too easily be perceived as criticism or blame.
7. It is important that you do not simply believe the feedback you receive, nor instantly reject it. It is that person's truth, their perceptions of you and your behaviour. Take it with you as a gift, live with it for a while, examine it, and if the cap fits, wear it.
8. One of the most reliable sources of understanding your own drives is the collective experience of a wide group of people. So get more feedback. Ask around, find out from a range of people how they see you. Different drives may predominate in different situations. Of course, there is always the possibility that they all share the same prejudices and give you a collective perception that is flawed. But in general, if a wide variety of people develops a consensus about your drives and predominant behaviour, they are usually worth listening to.
9. Examine your reactions to the feedback you get. Do you agree with it all or

do you protest? Which do you accept or reject? Which do you find familiar? Is there feedback about some of your behaviour or attitudes that you were unaware of?

 ## Summary

- In this chapter we have pulled together a lot of work you have done in the preceding chapters to develop three drives profiles:
    1. Your perceptions of the relative strengths of each drive within you.
    2. A measure of the drives that your work demands.
    3. An assessment of the drives you seek to satisfy through leisure interests.
- Using the 7Ps and 3LT helps to refine your understanding of yourself and other people.
- What you perceive in other people is dictated by who you are. Therefore a powerful way of gaining further insight into your own drives profile is to use others as a mirror with which to examine your own values.
- You can confirm or further develop your understanding of your drives by getting quality feedback from people around you.

CHAPTER 13

Making Changes – Vision to Action

In exploring your relationship to each of the 7Ps of drive you will have discovered which are your predominant ones, those that play the greatest part in shaping your hilltop and your approach to life. You may have also realised that there are some drives that you have not developed to any great extent, and possibly some that you would not wish to.

A phenomenon that we regularly observe in people is how predominance in any particular drive often produces a predictable reaction towards, or rejection of, one or more of the others. For example, someone who predominates strongly in the People drive predictably can perceive the Power drive as selfish and arrogant. This applies to any of the drives in their relationship to the others, whether it is a reaction to a drive in another person or a rejection of that drive within ourselves. We will examine this phenomenon in more detail later in this chapter, as it is often one of the root causes of personal limitations.

In Chapter 12 we asked you to develop a drives profile representing the relative predominances of the drives within you. We also asked you to develop a drives profile for the drives that your current work demands. Finally, we asked you to consider which drives you predominantly seek to satisfy via your interests outside work.

Frustrations in the workplace are often caused by work demanding that you operate in a drive state in which you personally feel uncomfortable. For example, some of us find selling or buying roles awkward. We may have to engage our Power drive to get the results needed, but don't feel right if it means we must get tough to close deals.

The question now, on the basis of the exploration you have done, is what changes do you want to make?

Your answer, of course, may be 'none'. Some of you will have read this book and felt it confirmed that you are in the right place, doing the right thing for you, and that no changes are needed. Others may recognise that although their work does not fulfil them totally, they are prepared to put up with it because it is worthwhile for other reasons – if they continue to seek fulfilment of their drives outside work. There may be others still who, while recognising their dissatisfaction, do not feel either ready, willing, or able at this time to bring about change.

And the changes some people need to make to get fulfilment in their roles could be beyond their ability to carry out. We understand that not all of us are able to make major changes in our organisation or in society at large, and we recognise that each of us has only a certain sphere of influence.

Nevertheless, we all do have *some* sphere of influence within which there are changes that we can make if we so wish, and we hold out the possibility that each of us can choose to improve the quality of our lives. Sometimes that might mean stretching the bounds of what we feel ourselves to be capable of, or making decisions that affect every facet of our being. In many situations, however, we can make major improvements in the quality of our lives by attending to the smallest of things. So, let us spell out some possible options, and then look more specifically at how to go about using them.

1. If your present work requires less of you than you feel you need to satisfy your more dominant drives, there are three basic alternatives:
   a) attempt to make changes in your existing role,
   b) look for a new job or career, or
   c) be content with your work and satisfy those drives elsewhere.
2. If your present work demands more in terms of certain drives than you presently manifest, you can choose a) or b) of the above or choose to engage in activities that will increase your capacity for the drives in question.
3. You may find that your current work is satisfactory, but in the light of your self-exploration, may wish to embark on a process of change aimed at personal development apart from work.

It is important to recognise that any change that we actively pursue will demand some form of conscious effort. With that effort will come, in most cases, the need to develop some knowledge, skills or awareness that we currently do not possess. In short, it is usually the case that any proactive change will require some personal commitment if it is to succeed.

The pre-requisite for change is commitment. Above all else, in order to make changes, people must want to do so. We are not talking about having to because there is simply no alternative, or about situations that change and therefore cause you to respond. Taking a conscious decision to change things requires an act of will, the commitment to say 'I *will* do it'. This applies whether we are setting about changing our present work situation, looking for another job, considering a total career change, or embarking on a path of personal development. Whilst each can bring enormous rewards, they can all be serious undertakings and are not to be taken lightly. Unless you are committed to the changes you wish to bring about, you are unlikely to succeed.

Commitment is not a feeling, it is an act of will. The decision to change anything is made only when we take action, when we actually do something about it. If we feel the urge to change, if we have a desire to do something different but do not act, then there is no commitment.

Change requires that we know who we are, where we want to be and how to get there. We need a clear, realistic assessment of our hilltop as a starting point, a clear image of what would fulfil us, and a strategy to bring both of those positions together. A good measure of your commitment to change, therefore, is to reflect on what effort you have so far put into using this book, or any other self-awareness methods, to explore your starting point.

 ### Self-awareness questions

How much time have you put into working with this book so far?
How much effort have you put into reflecting on the questions?
How comprehensive have your answers been?
How active have you been using 3LT with yourself and others?
What other self-awareness methods do you use?

It is not our intention to make readers feel admonished by the questions above. We feel the issue of commitment to be so important, however, that we need to be as clear about it as we can. Central to every change we will discuss is the notion of commitment.

Of course, we are all committed to something, even if we are not aware of it. We have described seven drive states and therefore types, each of which have at their deepest levels things that they value, believe in and are committed to. The third level of 3LT data of each type is a readout of their commitment. For a Plans type, the commitment is to order and structure, for a Positioning type it is harmony, and so on.

All of us are committed to the things we value. To generate the commitment to act, therefore, any changes we intend to make must be aligned with our deepest held values, i.e. with what we are committed to. To understand what those changes need to be, we need to understand what drives we seek to satisfy in the way we live our lives.

It comes back again to the central focus of this book – finding out what our true commitments are in order to be able to commit ourselves to their fulfilment. In our experience, it is incredibly difficult to get ourselves or anyone else to do anything that does not link in some way to 3LT third level commitments. For example, you may not feel inclined to go for a Sunday afternoon walk with your partner, but the commitment you have to maintaining harmony in the relationship may be enough to get you to go. You may feel little commitment to a task you have been given at work, but your commitment to always doing a good job, or maintaining your promotion prospects, leads you to get on with it. All this is 3LT third level activity.

 ## Exercise (take your time to do this one)

Examine your personal drives profile and, starting with your most predominant drives, list in descending order what you are committed to. Use your own words to express each of your drives. For example: 'I am deeply committed to having new experiences, intellectual challenge and the freedom to express myself', or 'I am committed to the search for meaning, harmony and peace'.

Find words that accurately express the levels of commitment you feel to the drives lower down your list.

Doing this exercise should highlight the things that you are committed to. These are the things that you are driven to satisfy and you need to use them as a benchmark against any changes you wish to make, no matter how large or small.

We have repeatedly stated that the reasons for engaging in any activity or behaviour can only be understood by looking at the drives or motivations behind that behaviour. Every micro event in our lives is governed at a macro level by the core of our hilltop, our values and commitments. Our drives are expressions of those commitments seeking fulfilment.

Micro changes need to be aligned to your macro commitments. Macro issues are basically life changes, i.e. 'What I want to do with my life', or 'My overall purpose'. Micro level issues might be 'What I want to do today' or 'What I want to get out of this particular activity'. At the macro level we can use words like Purpose and Mission; at the micro level they become Goals and Objectives.

Both micro and macro changes are expressions of our commitments, and both have their roots in the starting place for any change – our Purpose drive. *An act of will is purposeful behaviour, and any successful change must begin by focusing on Purpose.*

We also need to be clear about what change really means. Change is a *process*, not an event. It is impossible to deal in any detail with the infinite number of possible changes that those reading this book may wish to make. Each one of us has our own unique situation, our individual needs and particular things that we would like to be different. The common factor is that change can be seen as a *process*, and tackled as such. If we understand a process for change, we can use it to address our own unique issues. We call this process *Vision to Action.*

Different people approach change in different ways. Some will resist change or need to mitigate against every possible risk rather than step into the unknown. Others will suddenly resign from a secure job and walk away, prepared to deal with whatever problems might ensue.

Your approach to change, like everything else, will be dictated by your hilltop. In Chapter 12 we discussed the idea of using feedback as a mirror with which to recognise our true selves. This idea holds true not only for the way we perceive and interact with other people, but for the way in which we make things happen. In the process of making things happen, bringing about the changes we desire, we will need to be aware of and overcome our own preferences and limitations as much as the real obstacles we perceive that might stand in our way.

Throughout the descriptions of the various drive states we have been careful to use the word 'limitations' rather than 'weaknesses'. This is more than a semantic difference: drives are not intrinsically weak. What we have experienced over the years is that predominance in one drive usually leads to lack of attention in some of the others. The limitations we have described throughout the drive chapters are indications of what predictably will be missing in the behaviour of each type, rather than weaknesses of the particular drive in question. So, when it comes to each of us attempting consciously to change things, we inevitably will confront our own limitations around the drives we engage the least.

Vision to Action: stages and the 7Ps

Vision to Action is a process model that features a step-by-step approach to change. It acknowledges that for each of us, some of the steps will play to our strengths and seem easy, while others will seem difficult. A process that does not take such individual differences into account is not viable, in our opinion. Before applying Vision to Action to the changes that you may wish to make, we need to describe the process and some of the potential blocks to success.

Vision to Action draws on the 7P model to create a way of understanding the components of bringing about change. It is based on the following premises:

1. Our lives are creative acts. They are expressions of how we translate our visions into action. Whether aware of it or not, we are all attempting to fulfil our visions.
2. Change is a creative act. It is the 'real-isation', the 'making real', of an imagined future state.
3. In translating a vision which starts initially in the imagination – Purpose – into something tangible – Product – we need to address certain issues and activities that will determine the level of its success.
4. These issues and activities correspond to the different drive states within us and can be described using the 7P model.

To summarise, we can use the same 7P model in two new ways when attempting to change things. The 7Ps of Vision to Action is a checklist for moving an idea from Purpose to Product. The 7Ps of Drive is a way of looking at the strengths and limitations of the person and how these can block or inhibit the change process. The order changes.

The 7P action stages of Vision to Action come in the following sequence:

7P Action Stages – Vision to Action

1. Purpose	Develop a clear vision of what you want to achieve
2. Positioning	Check it for appropriateness and feasibility
3. Plans	Develop a strategic plan of action
4. Power	Commit yourself and your resources to it
5. Process	Sort out an order of doing things
6. People	Engage your own and other people's energies
7. Product	Persevere until you achieve a measurable outcome

Whether you are contemplating a major life decision, a role change or even an attempt to influence your boss, you can use this model to structure your approach in the changes you wish to make. The problems we observe people having in working through this as a process (or any other process) arise from the tendency to pay undue attention to some stages, and skip over or dismiss certain others as irrelevant. In understanding this process and the pitfalls that you may encounter when approaching change, you need to be aware of your drive profile – which drives predominate and particularly, your least dominant drives.

We have used Vision to Action and the 7Ps of Drive for many years to help the owners of small businesses bring about necessary changes. In such a situation, the business is a total mirror of the person running it.

We dealt with some owners who would not, or could not, sit down and do the work needed to plan and organise; some who had wonderful products but who could not assert themselves in a selling situation; others who had a great idea but had no concept of finding out if there was a demand for it, and so on.

In every case, this inability or unwillingness to engage across the spectrum of drives produced corresponding difficulties in the business. In the examples above, some became totally disorganised, others unable to generate enough sales, while some ended up developing products that no-one wanted to buy.

Vision to Action: blocks to success

We will now take a look at the 7Ps as they apply in Vision to Action, focussing particularly on what *blocks* success.

1. Purpose

• What are you trying to achieve?
• What is the vision of where you want to be?
• What are the commitments you are trying to fulfil?

This is the arena of those who have strong Purpose drives, who are inspired by playing with images. It is the stage of the process where new ideas get generated and worked with enthusiastically. They are then developed, improved and further clarified, leading to a strong, clear *vision* of the end product or situation.

This is the beginning of any process of change – we need to know what we are aiming at if we are to point our activities in the right direction. It is also the stage which many of us find the most difficult, especially when we are pondering the macro question of our purpose in life. There are no hard facts, no details to anchor ourselves to. Sometimes an image is difficult to describe in words, which is why many approaches to vision-building include other forms of self-expression. The smaller the task in hand, the easier the process seems to become.

If your personal drive profile shows that you feel little identity with this drive, your difficulty in generating a clear vision about where you want to be may make this stage uncomfortable. A limitation at this level usually causes a person to adopt other people's visions, or in refusing to suspend critical assessment of any ideas that are generated. This leads, inevitably, to accepting only that which already exists, and therefore dismissing other possibilities.

It is sometimes the case that an individual has more than a limitation in a particular drive: they may actually have a *negative* attitude about the work that needs to be done in some stages of this process. This can cause blockage for the person at that stage, rather than his or her simply not being very good at it but willing to try.

The block to successful change at this level, therefore, may show up as clearly avoiding image-creating work or repeatedly creating new ideas but dismissing them as impossibilities and never taking them further. The vision remains here unless it is progressed to the next stage.

2. Positioning

- Here the vision needs to be put into *context*, i.e. is this the right time and place for it?
- Is there a window of opportunity?
- Is it really appropriate for me?
- Is it feasible?
- What are the wider implications of this?
- How will my vision of change affect other factors in my life?

In the business world, this is market research, an attempt to be sensitive enough to the marketplace to be appropriate with a product or a service. It is also the realm of feasibility assessments. Checking that a vision is feasible may mean that all the other areas of the 7Ps need research during this stage as preparation before developing a strategy. For example, you will need to understand any Power issues, what resources will be needed, etc. or what People issues – in terms of other perspectives – need to be considered.

At the level of individual change, it is essential to consider your vision and yourself in the widest context. This level of the change process adds foresight and appropriateness. What is needed is the Positioning drive's qualities of sensitivity and sense of integration. If your drives profile shows little evidence of this drive, your vision may bring more difficulties than rewards. If you skip a thorough investigation at this level of the process, then the changes you bring about may have many unforeseen consequences. There are many fine examples of how a lack of foresight has brought products into the market place that no-one wanted, or projects that have been undertaken which have had an unforeseen environmental impact.

A block here can be a solid refusal to acknowledge inappropriateness, and an unwillingness to subject the vision to scrutiny by oneself or others.

3. Plans

• Further progress requires good *organisation,* i.e. how am I going to achieve it?
• What do I need to do?
• How am I going to translate the vision into a strategy for action?
• How am I to measure my success?

At this stage the change can be clearly conceptualised and broad strategic plans produced. The vision can be put on paper in the form of an action plan and can readily be explained to others. It is the work of the Plans drive, accounting for the many variables that need to be considered and developing ways of tackling them.

In some changes that are envisaged, there will clearly be risk, or at least the need to plan how to generate resources. In a business sense, the product of this stage of the process is the document that you might need to show to your bank manager.

For those of us who dislike planning as an activity, this stage can be boring, tedious or extremely difficult. Remember, however, that a limitation in your ability to engage the Plans drive will lead to fundamental disorganisation with all the attendant difficulties.

A block at this level shows as an unwillingness or refusal to get down to some solid planning, or to think through a series of options and their consequences.

4. Power

The most elegant of plans will stay on the shelf unless they are *energised.* Ask yourself:

• Do I have the necessary confidence?
• Am I ready, willing and able to put the plans into operation?
• Do I have the commitment to make it happen?
• Am I willing to take any necessary risk with my resources?

This stage requires a dynamic injection of energy in the form of personal commitment and willpower. Until this point, the work involved in the process has required little risk or commitment. This, essentially, is the decision point, the fulcrum of Vision to Action, and it demands confidence. It can also demand some form of commitment of resources – usually money. So for those of us who are not comfortable in the Power drive, where does confidence come from? You can gain a lot of confidence by paying attention to each stage of this process, checking things as thoroughly as you can. Over-confidence often signals a person who has not been willing to do the necessary preparation.

Being limited in your access to the Power drive can result in lack of commitment, lack of confidence and an unwillingness to take some risks.

A block at this level may show as refusing to stick your neck out or compete, or to get out and sell yourself. Without this injection of energy, the changes you desire will not happen.

5. Process

For the vision to be put into action, the plans need to be broken into some linear *sequence*.

- Where do I start?
- In which order should I do things in?
- How will I know if I am on the right path?
- How flexible can I be if things change?
- What timescale shall I set myself?

Careful analysis of what needs to be done will enable serialisation – scheduling the many pieces of the jigsaw into the best operational order. This stage demands great flexibility as the linear plan has to adapt to many factors. In any change situation, some things are best done before others. It is useful, for example, to have bought the new tiles before you start stripping the old ones off the roof. The more complex the situation, the greater the need for the skills and qualities of the Process drive – analysis and adaptability.

A limitation at this level can result in the right things being done, but in the wrong order. In business it results in poor project scheduling or cash flow management. A limitation in this drive can also result in an inability to change the plan if it is not working.

A block at this level can be a refusal to do any in-depth analysis or monitoring of patterns and results.

6. People

At this point the process will stick unless energy is put in to *mobilise* it. Ask yourself:

- Can I get going right now?
- Can I make the first move?

- Do I have the enthusiasm to put this into operation?
- Who am I going to talk to about it today?

This is the stage of enthusiasm: getting the change process into action starts here. It requires the vitality and energy to get on with it, or to go out and engage other people. Because many of the changes may have an effect on others, or need to be agreed by others, this stage of the process demands the ability to include other people in the vision. It is of little use developing a wonderful plan for change if you are unable to gain the necessary agreement of others.

If the People drive is not strong in you, then at this stage of the process the limitation will be in establishing good rapport in working relationships. In general, people will engage with you to the degree that they like you: most of us prefer doing things with and for people we get on with.

A block at this level may be a refusal to develop good relationships with people, remaining purely task-oriented. A block here may also manifest itself as lethargy or procrastination rather than the enthusiasm to get on with it.

7. Product

This stage of the process demands having the stamina to *produce* the vision as a physical reality. Ask yourself:

- How persistent can I be?
- What will make me give up?
- How effective am I being?
- Could I do more?

This stage demands that the necessary skills, strength and stamina be put to work. It demands that we recognise that change needs effort. It may mean burning the midnight oil, it may mean persisting in the face of adversity. It could entail going to several meetings every day for weeks in order to gain some movement. Whatever the change, it will usually mean that you need a degree of health and fitness to produce it.

For those of us who do not identify much with the Product drive, the limitation is essentially one of stamina. At this level of the process it could mean that the effort would soon run out of steam and collapse, or simply would not have the physical resources to cope.

A block at this level can show as laziness, or reluctance to get your hands dirty.

Self-awareness questions

Do you understand clearly the commitments you need to satisfy?

Do you know what changes you need to make to do this?

Do you know where your potential limitations are to achieving success?

 ## Summary

- To bring about changes that will improve the quality of our lives, we need to know who we are, where we want to be and how to get there.
- We need to commit ourselves to action that will bring about the desired changes.
- Any changes, large or small, need to be linked to satisfying our drives – the things we are committed to at the deepest level.
- Our drives profile is a readout of our deepest commitments, the third level in 3LT. Change is a process and should be dealt with as such.
- Vision to Action is a way of describing how a change can be planned and implemented, bringing change from an image into concrete action.
- The stages of Vision to Action mirror the qualities and characteristics of the 7Ps of drive.
- Our predominances and relative lack of engagement in certain drives will affect how we approach the process of change.
- This will show up as a preference for certain stages in the process and a limitation or avoidance of the work required in others.
- The net result will be measured in how successful we are in translating our vision into reality.

CHAPTER 14

Change Through Communication – Influencing Others

Almost all of us live in a complex web of relationships. Both in and out of work there are people whom we, in some way, are affected by or affect. Most attempts to change, at some point therefore, have to be communicated to other people.

At the People stage of Vision to Action, our plans for making any particular change emerge from inside our heads to cross the chasm between us and the people we need to engage. Without the ability to communicate effectively with these people, our chances of success can be slim. It may be a boss we need to communicate with to negotiate a more satisfying role, or a group involved in making a change in the way we want to structure our approach to work. It may be our partner we need to include in our thinking, because of the direct effects any changes may have on him or her. Communication is such a central part of life that it deserves a book of its own, so we will restrict ourselves to discussing the role of communication in the process of achieving change.

Communication is often defined as a two-way process – the giving and receiving of information between people. The question that inevitably occurs to us is 'Are we really communicating or are we simply exchanging information?'

When we really communicate we reach a point where we have a common understanding and perspective over a particular point. There are, however, countless situations where we are engaged in conversation but are not actually communicating with the other person. They have their views, we have ours, and little attempt is made to bridge the gap between the two hilltops. Watch politicians discussing things – they rarely attempt to communicate with each other.

Communication and change

Communicating with a view to changing things almost always involves some form of influencing or persuasion. If we have the power to disregard the views of others, we can take the route of simply informing people of our decisions. However, even in these situations, gaining agreement and support is usually far more productive than gaining compliance and resistance.

The way most people attempt to influence or persuade others looks to us as though they are standing on their hilltops with their fingers in their ears. It is as though people believe they must get their point across, defend their position and argue that their perspective is the right one. In their desire to gain agreement most people seem to treat the other person's perspective much as a salesperson might when he or she is handling objections. They do not listen, or at least listen only to select those parts of the message that they can use to their own advantage.

Communication involves temporarily leaving our own hilltop. If we really want to communicate with someone we must listen. We must listen well enough to be able to speak in a way that is both understandable and meaningful to the other person. We must be prepared to come down from our own hilltop, cross the valley and stand as much as possible on the other person's hilltop, to see the world from their point of view. Only then will we be able to enhance our communication.

Influencing and persuasion means gaining the commitment of other people to a certain course of action. Gaining people's commitment is a subject that has occupied management thinking for a long time. The only way to get people to do things they do not value is by using some degree of coercive power: with a gun to their heads, most people will do most things. However, as all the research into such methods demonstrates, coercion gains *compliance,* not *commitment.* And in many situations we might wish to change, we will not have coercive power – we will *have to* use our ability to communicate.

Our approach to influencing is based on the following simple ideas:

1. You cannot simply broadcast from your hilltop and expect others to see your point of view.
2. Most people have their own perspectives which are valid for them.
3. Most people resist being influenced if it means giving up their point of view.
4. People are more easily influenced if their needs, commitments and perspectives are included rather than excluded.

To influence people successfully, you need to know enough about how they view the situation and therefore how their perspectives might be included. You also need to know what their commitments are if you are going to talk in ways that are meaningful to them. It means that in using Vision to Action as a way of structuring your approach to change, you may have to do some reflection or research on the people you will have to influence.

Take, for example, a manager whom you want to influence. Let's say you are not fulfilled in the way your job is presently organised and want to persuade your manager to allow you to do it differently. You may be able to develop a clear image of the changes that you want to bring about. However, in establishing whether it *is* a realistic or achievable goal, you will need to assess it in relation to the person whose agreement you need.

People agree with things that are linked to their own commitments. *To successfully influence someone, you need to find a way of linking what you want with what they are committed to. You must bear in mind at all times that the reasons why you want the changes may have no meaning for them whatsoever.* Unless you can make the change meaningful in their terms rather than yours, you are likely to fail.

To continue with the manager example, he or she is more likely to agree to changes if the value to them can be seen from where he or she stands. This is not to imply that managers in general are not concerned with their staff's fulfilment. If they are, and that is part of their hilltop, your proposal for change can be linked with their commitment to see staff members fulfilled. If they are not, then you need to find out what their commitment is in order to link to it.

Influencing as a process with the 7Ps

In the last chapter we described change as a process, not an event. The same holds true for influencing. There is much to be gained from treating most of our influencing attempts as a process to be attended to rather than a series of spontaneous, unplanned outbursts. In this way, you can picture influencing as a sequence of questions to deal with.

You can use the Vision to Action model as a way of preparing and implementing a change process, no matter what the specific change might be. Without committing yourself to making any proposals at this stage, you can consider various issues against the 7P profile as follows:

Purpose   Can I clearly describe what I want to achieve?
Positioning Can I assess the feasibility and appropriateness of the goal?
Plans   Can I develop a strategy for achieving it?
Power   Can I assess what power I need and where to get it?
Process   Can I serialise it into a plan of action?
People   Can I establish what will influence the people involved?
Product   Can I develop clear measures of success?

In our work on the role of communication in the influencing process, we have found that to influence someone you must first prepare as thoroughly as possible. Secondly, you need to get into a position in which you can understand the context of your proposed changes more fully – the more you know, the greater your chances of success. Such a position should also enable you to be listened to when you do propose any changes.

Establishing such a position means developing rapport, credibility and trust with the person you are trying to influence. Successful influencing does not begin with confronting people cold, it needs an appropriate level of relationship.

This, of course, brings us back to the notion of hilltops and types. Developing rapport, credibility and trust means exhibiting behaviour, attitudes and concerns that the other person values.

 Self-awareness questions

What do people need to exhibit with you to develop rapport, credibility and trust?
Conversely, what do people exhibit that has the opposite effect?
Which of the drives do your answers belong to?

By now we hope you will have become familiar enough with the 7P map to be able to generate what each type will need to experience from you if you are to build an appropriate level of relationship. But here are some predictable behaviours, attitudes and concerns that we have consistently found each type needs from you if they are to form a working relationship.

Purpose	Enthusiasm, openness to creative ideas, willingness to talk about problems and possibilities
Positioning	Sensitivity, awareness, willingness to share deeply, a sense of harmony and integrity in the relationship
Plans	Clear conceptual thinking, ability to order your thoughts, be precise and thorough
Power	Self-confidence, energy, commitment to make things happen, willingness to take risks
Process	Intellectual brightness, new perspectives and ideas, capacity to be flexible and responsive to change
People	Sociability, concern for others, willingness to co-operate and do a good job
Product	Pragmatism, common sense, willingness to buckle down to hard work, stamina

The danger of listing predictabilities in this way is that they become simplistic. We have included these as core needs, but in reality there are an almost infinite number of ways in which these needs express themselves in interactions, ranging from the Power type who will test your mettle within the first few minutes to check your self-confidence, to the People type who will offer you a cup of coffee or tea before getting down to business. You need to respond appropriately to both.

We were presenting a programme design to a new client, a very bright Plans type. As we were talking through the design, he would regularly stop and ask 'Why are you doing that exercise there?' or 'What is the objective?', etc.

He could not judge our credibility on our techniques and models, of which he had limited knowledge, and was therefore demanding that we articulate the logic and rationale behind the shape of the programme. If we could, then we passed the test.

So, if you build a good working relationship with someone, they are usually much more open to being influenced than if you have none. However, developing such a relationship will not in itself provide you with all you need in order to influence, it will simply provide a platform from which you can gather enough information with which to develop an influencing strategy.

Earlier, we mentioned the central role of commitment in the influencing process. The idea is that we need to find legitimate ways of linking our proposals for change to what we know the person to be committed to. The questions we therefore need answers to are:

• What do I know about this person?
• What are the significant issues involved in this change for him or her?
• What might be his or her perspective and objections?
• What is his or her predominant drive and therefore commitments?
• What will I have to include in these changes that he or she can agree to?

Every time you speak with someone you are exchanging potentially valuable information. Having a degree of rapport, credibility and trust allows the quality of information to increase and allows you to ask the deeper questions of the Three Level Technique (3LT) – which might otherwise remain unasked. Respecting and valuing a person's responses to those deeper questions is a very powerful way of deepening a relationship in its own right.

A word of warning. If you are to be successful in achieving change, you must have in your criteria for success the requirement that both you and other people who are affected by the change are happy with it – in essence that you achieve a win-win situation. If you achieve a win-lose conclusion, then you are more likely to have *manipulated* than *influenced*, and you will almost certainly pay the cost in other ways.

So, what might be the commitments of managers (or anyone else) that you may need to link your proposals to? The following are examples of what the different types might need in any change proposals in order to link with their intrinsic commitments:

Purpose types   Need to feel that the changes are innovative and creative and aimed at solving problems that will move them or you closer to realising a vision.

Positioning types   Need to feel that the changes are thoughtful, widely considered and appropriate, that they will integrate and build rather than separate and divide.

Plans types   Need to feel that the changes are rational, logically justifiable and can be done without bending the rules or causing much disorganisation.

Power types   Need to feel that the changes will be more profitable or efficient and will in some way add to, rather than subtract from, their own status.

Process types   Need to feel that the changes can withstand intellectual scrutiny and open up the possibility of new ways of doing things.

People types   Need to feel that the changes are in everyone's best interest, will improve morale and co-operation and will not disaffect others.

Product types   Need to feel that the changes make practical sense and improve efficiency and output in a pragmatic and measurable way.

Of course, in every situation there will be specific concerns that will need to be understood and taken into account. There may be very good reasons why, even if the changes link directly with his or her commitments, a manager cannot agree to your proposals. There may be pressure on him or her that prevents allowing the changes, or to do so may have consequences that you cannot foresee because you do not see the whole picture. We cannot be specific about every situation – only you can add the complexities that are unique to your context.

Another word of caution. The linkage to what this person is committed to needs to be real and justifiable, not pretend. If you are proposing a change to a Power type on the grounds that it will be more profitable when in reality it will not, you will lose credibility at the very least. If you pretend to a People type that the changes are for the benefit of all when in fact it is only you that will benefit, you will severely damage your relationship. The fly-by-night salesperson may get away with such pretence on a one-off sale, but for any ongoing relationship it is a dangerous practice – it destroys precisely the foundations upon which successful communication, and therefore influencing, is built.

The difficulty of communication

Knowing theoretically how to communicate and being able to do so can be two very different things. *When we attempt to communicate with someone else, we are inevitably confronted by our own hilltop.*

So how do we communicate with someone who has a world view that we do not share? How do we make sense to a hilltop that is governed by a drive that we have very little access to within ourselves? To give an example, how do we structure our thoughts, ideas and language in a way that will connect with someone who is Plans-driven, when we find rational argument and logic alien to the more emotional world that we inhabit? How do we communicate in a sensitive and meaningful way to someone when we ourselves do not feel the need for sensitivity?

Communicating with people who have very different outlooks on life compared to your own is of course the fundamental difficulty in all human interaction. In relationships at work, with your partner, between parents and children, between groups, classes or races, bridging the chasm between different perspectives is a constant problem. The difficulty is often compounded in situations when you are actively seeking to exert influence on others as opposed to simply getting on with them.

Getting on with people raises another issue worthy of mention at this point: improving the quality of relationships may be a change that many of us would like to make to help our work to be more rewarding than it presently is. For many of us, a major frustration of work is that we can rarely choose whom we work with. Consequently, we can end up working with people with whom we find little in common.

Much of the work we do as a consultancy within organisations involves improving the quality of relationships between people. In every case this eventually focuses on the ability to understand and communicate. We teach 3LT, listening, questioning, the 7Ps: all are aimed essentially at raising the participants' awareness of the different hilltops that individuals inhabit and, more than that, at making each participant aware of their responsibilities in the equation that is the basis of any interaction.

If you want to communicate with people and improve the quality of the relationship between you or influence them, then ultimately it is *your* responsibility to do so. Do not expect the other person to change – you must do the changing.

The reasons for failure to develop relationships with people are many. We often fail to appreciate or value their perspectives, do not share their attitudes or beliefs, or do not speak the same language (sometimes literally!). In short we may feel that they are not 'our kind of people'. And yet, it is our own hilltop that governs what we appreciate, what we value, etc. It is where our own hilltop is that determines how far away others are from it. If we had equal access to all of our drive states we could more readily appreciate them in others. We could respect and value the physical skills of the Product type, the concern and care of the People type, the intellectual capacity of the Process type, and so on. To the extent that we can enter each drive within us, we can understand the hilltops of others and talk the language of those worlds.

 Self-awareness questions

Reflect on your drives profile.
Which of the drives do you engage most and least?
Which types do you relate to best?
Which do you find the most difficulty with?

Developing our ability to communicate is essential if we want to increase our capacity to bring about changes. Being able to communicate with a wide range of people means being able to engage the corresponding drives within us. If we cannot do this, we may be perceived by others as not their kind of people.

Operating in unfamiliar, potentially threatening areas in attempting to communicate is a very powerful vehicle for self-development. Demanding that others come to our hilltop so that we communicate means that we do not have to do the work, and also that they are assuming the responsibility for the relationship.

Exercise

Can you identify a specific change that you want to bring about in your work situation? If so, work through it using the Vision to Action process thoroughly. Make sure you pay attention to a full assessment at the Positioning stage before moving on.

Start with a small change first – nothing succeeds like success.

Summary

- Most changes involve communicating with others.
- Communication means reaching a common understanding or perspective.
- Communicating about change usually involves influencing and persuasion.
- Influencing means getting the commitment of the other person.
- People agree with things that are in some way linked to their commitments.
- Different types have different commitments.
- Influencing, like change, can be understood as a process.
- Vision to Action can be used to prepare for and implement change.
- Influencing requires an appropriate level of relationship to support it.
- Relationships are built through rapport, credibility and trust.
- Different types look for different qualities in relationships.
- We need to assume full responsibility for the quality of our relationships.
- The more we understand, the better our chances of success.
- The ability to communicate is governed by our hilltop preferences.
- Learning to communicate with a wide range of people almost always involves effort and personal development.

CHAPTER 15

Changing Jobs and Careers

You may now want a new job in your present company or a new one, or embark on a new career, having decided that no amount of change to your current job will be enough to fulfil you. Many people find themselves moving along a career path when they discover that given the choice, they would take a different route. Others are in fields of work that have changed so dramatically over the years that they bear little resemblance to the kind of work that first attracted them.

People approach changing jobs or taking new directions in their work in many different ways. There are those whose total job-count exceeds their age, who move in and out of different companies doing more or less the same kind of work wherever they go. There are others whose career profile has no apparent connectedness, who every few years seem to make a major leap into a very different field. At the other end of the scale there are others who have been in the same job with the same company since they finished their education.

It is impossible to generalise about who gets the most fulfilment without exploring individual motivations. What does need acknowledging is that such changes can be much bigger events in some people's lives than in others. The decision to look for another job or change our field of work presents us all with the opportunity to engage in a purposeful activity. For most of us who spend the major part of our waking day involved with work activity, it is an opportunity to make that activity more fulfilling than it presently is.

The purpose of a job or career change should be that of seeking great self-fulfilment. The essential questions to be addressed in changing a job or career are:

- What will fulfil me?
- What do I have to offer?
- Where will my needs be met?

What will fulfil me?

The work you have done throughout this book should have clearly identified what you as an individual need for your fulfilment. The drives you have are the expression of seeking to achieve the things you value. Any change of job or career needs to be directly connected to the greater fulfilment of your drives.

Exercise

Referring to your drive profile, make a prioritised list of the needs that any new job or career must fulfil.

The list made in the previous exercise is your Purpose – the backdrop to which you will constantly need to refer in any of the changes that you embark upon. At this point, do you have a clear image of what you have to do to fulfil your drives? If not, it is the time to do some envisioning. It is very frustrating to know that you want to do something different but not to know what *it* is.

 Exercise

Picture yourself in two, five or ten years time. Imagine that you have succeeded in finding or creating a perfectly fulfilling situation, one that is all you would wish for.

Describe the picture in as much detail as you can. What are you doing? What does the work involve? How do you spend your day? What sort of environment are you in? How are you dressed? Where do you live?

Envisioning is a strange activity for many. Some call it wishful thinking, others feel it is daydreaming. In our experience it is neither. If you need to be convinced of the power of the imagination, re-read the Purpose chapter. Our imagination, more than anything else, governs what we are and what we can become. If we do not hold the possibility in our imagination, then it *is* impossible.

An image is not a goal, not something that is likely to be stated in a sentence. Sometimes a full-blown image or vision can quite literally drop into your head, and you suddenly can see very clearly where you want to be. However, those happenings are rare. In doing the last exercise you may have only been able to grasp tiny fragments of your ideal future: growing an image into something of substance can take time. The best way we have found of helping it along is to pay attention to it. That means feeding it with possibilities, rejecting nothing initially, reading about how others live, watching documentaries, listening to people, asking them questions about what their work involves, finding out what interests them about it. The more you allow into your imagination, the fuller the image that will grow, and the wider the possibilities will become.

What do I have to offer?

There are thousands of jobs or careers that can potentially satisfy each drive, and it may take some dedicated research on your part to home in on some particular ones. Understanding your abilities, in terms of the range of skills that you possess, may help.

Your drive profile cannot necessarily be used as a reliable indicator of your skill level. We know people, for example, who are totally competent in the skills of planning and organising but who do not have a corresponding level of Plans drive. Similarly, there are people we meet who, although being predominantly Power-driven, are in reality very unskilful in their attempts to satisfy this drive.

 Exercise

Make a list of all the jobs you have ever done. Itemise the skills you have developed in each, using your own words to describe them in as much detail as you can.

If you take time to fully explore the skills you have, including the ones you do not currently use much, you may be surprised at the range you possess.

Frequently, when people do this exercise as part of a curriculum vitae, they comment that it actually does not sound like them at all. This is probably because it brings into awareness those attributes that are not a conscious part of the person's self-image. Once again, it is a very powerful way of feeding the central image and opening up possibilities.

Where will my needs be met?

In the final analysis, all the work you have done on understanding your drives and skills, and developing a clear image of the kind of work you want to be doing, leads to the question of where to find the job or career that will meet your needs.

You may be at a stage where you have a very clear idea of the role that you would want, and even the organisations that might provide it. On the other hand, you may only have the ingredients, and need to search for the role that contains them.

It is beyond the scope of this book to cover all the practical aspects of job-hunting or career change, and there are already some excellent books on these subjects. What we are concerned with are the less practical but essential aspects of finding a situation which fulfils your predominant drives.

Making judgments

Many of you may have had the experience of applying for and getting a job, with very little prior exposure to its finer details – the working environment, culture, new colleagues, etc. Sometimes things work out well, but often they do not. The net result can be a severe waste of time for both employee and employer.

It is *your* responsibility to check out as thoroughly as possible any job for which you apply, or any career you embark upon. Applying to an organisation for a job means that you are considering entering into a relationship which may last for many years, and one which will certainly involve much of your time and energy. Before being able to commit yourself to a decision, you need to engage in a process by which you can evaluate the benefits of that relationship.

This means understanding what opportunities exist within the role or the company for fulfilling your drives. Which of your skills does the role actually demand? What sort of environment will you be entering? What are the cultural expectations and norms within the company? What are the people like? Through the work you have done so far, you can generate a thorough series of questions that will enable you to determine the extent to which this role or company is one that can satisfy your needs. Through the use of a job-hunting manual, you can develop ways of gathering a lot of the information that you will need to assist you in making a judgment about a particular job, career or company.

Interviews

The classic interview is often not the ideal situation in which to glean the information you need. In some of our personal interview experiences, the most we saw of the company was the reception area, the inside of the interview room and a personnel officer's perception of the role on offer. Some of you may have been more fortunate and experienced more enlightened interview methods. But whatever the quality, we suggest that in order to make an informed judgment, you need a wider exposure than an interview.

The interview is necessary in letting a company tell you what is on offer and what it is looking for from you. It needs to assess your suitability, and this is also an opportunity for you to tell it what you want it to know about you.

But you also may require a walk around the workplace, meeting and talking to people – particularly those doing a similar job to the one you have applied for. We recognise that there may be difficulties in this. For example, few companies would like you to talk to your predecessor if he or she has been sacked. However, if you do not find a way of researching what you are perhaps about to say yes to, then you relinquish the ability to make an informed judgment.

The interview is one of the few situations (apart from the law courts) where the declared purpose is to judge. Some people thrive in interview situations, others hate them. Some interviewers are excellent, others poor. The question we need to ask is 'On what basis are you being judged?'

There is plenty of evidence to suggest that hiring decisions are often made within the first few minutes of an interview, with the rest of the time being spent corroborating the decision. Even if that is not the case and judgment is suspended until the end, what are the criteria for your selection or otherwise? It comes down to two basic things: the requirements of the job and the company, and the person doing the interviewing.

Job descriptions vary enormously. Some are thin, factual descriptions, others break down the role into specific tasks, functions and skills required. Some even state the drives that are needed in the job in question, for example, 'Applicants must have excellent communication, coaching, counselling and people skills' or 'Must be dynamic, self-motivated and welcome personal challenge'.

Some companies put applicants through rigorous aptitude tests, assessment centres and a whole battery of inventories to establish suitability against these criteria. Having a series of applicants, all suitable, with the skills required and all dynamic, self-motivated and so on, how is the final judgment to be made? On what other grounds does the interviewer choose one candidate over the equally qualified others?

In many instances, all things being equal, the final decision is made at an emotional level. The interviewer may have a feeling that you are 'our kind of person', that you will fit well within the culture or even that your appearance is particularly acceptable. A host of value decisions may be made about your qualities and attributes above and beyond the formal requirements of the job – *the important point to recognise is that they are made from the interviewer's hilltop.*

Being interviewed is, of course, a communication situation. More than that, it is a situation where you are actively attempting to influence a decision in your favour. An interviewer may want to know why you want a job with that company, what you have to offer, whether you will fit in and on what conditions you would accept the job. You will want to know what the job entails, if it will fulfil your needs and utilise your skills, whether it has an environment which you would enjoy and how you can convince them to hire you.

It is very important that the interview is a two-way situation rather than an interrogation. If you are passive, you will not find out what you need to know and – equally important – you will not have the opportunity of uncovering anything about the interviewer's hilltop. If you don't get the interviewer talking you will not have a chance to listen. If you do not have a chance to listen you will not gain the understanding you need and will be unable to speak in ways that are meaningful to the interviewer. You will try to mention every conceivable benefit you offer, almost at random, hoping that at least one might connect with his or her hilltop.

If the final decision that singles you out from the rest is to be made on subjective data and impressions, then your ability to identify and connect with the other person's hilltop is the major factor. The job may very clearly demand the qualities and attributes of the Power type, for example, but you may be being interviewed by a People type. If you are not aware of this, you may easily overplay your hand and be seen as too aggressive. You will need to balance the display of your Power drive with some humility and signs of concern for others.

 ## Summary

- The purpose of changing a job or a career is to seek greater self-fulfilment.
- The basic questions are: What will fulfil me? What do I have to offer? Where will my needs be met?
- The backdrop to any new job or career is the drives that you seek to fulfil.
- Developing a clear vision usually takes time, commitment and effort.
- Itemising the skills you possess will increase your options.
- Skill levels may not be directly correlated to your drive predominances.
- It is worth reading and using a specific job-hunter's manual.
- You will need to research thoroughly in order to make an informed judgment about a role, career or potential employer.
- An interview is an influencing situation.
- Beyond being suitably qualified, there is a host of subjective criteria which may be used by an interviewer.
- You must be able to identify, understand and communicate with the interviewer's hilltop.
- An interview must be a two-way process.

CHAPTER 16

Change Through Personal Development

Self-development and self-fulfilment go hand in hand.

This is not to say that self-development *is* self-fulfilment, although for many people that is the case – working towards actualising their full potential is their way of striving for self-fulfilment. For others, it is a question of ends and means.

We cannot expect to get where we want to be, i.e. to fulfil ourselves, without effort. Things that we can do without effort do not develop us. An athlete does not develop strength, stamina or technique without effort. Whatever we do that stretches us also develops us. Putting effort into things that we want to learn or achieve is a form of self-development.

Much has been written about personal development over the last 40 years. Much of it has come to be synonymous with spiritual growth and a quest for inner knowledge. While we acknowledge and include these within our understanding of personal development, we would not want to confine our definition to only these realms. Personal development is not only continued growth in our predominant drives, but active nourishment of our least dominant ones. It is the process of nurturing and developing our ability to operate effectively across the spectrum of drives.

We have asked you to do a good deal of work in reading this book, reflecting on the predominances of the various drives within your own make-up. The irony of self-fulfilment seems to us to be that in order to satisfy our dominant drives, we need to engage some or all of the others. We know for example that it takes more than sheer guts and determination to succeed, more than a meaningful intent to make something happen. We are all attempting to live out our visions, but to be successful – to be self-fulfilled – we need creativity, foresight, organisation, confidence, adaptability, sociability and stamina. In short, we need access to the 7Ps of drive functioning effectively within us.

If you examine any unsuccessful project against the 7P profile, it will have failed or blocked at one or more points on the way. Perhaps the original idea was ill-conceived, or there were unforeseen mitigating factors. Perhaps it was badly organised, lacked resources or determination or wasn't systematic enough. Perhaps people were not interested, or it ran out of steam.

Personal development means working on our ability to engage the appropriate drive when it is needed. Our limitations (and we have met very few people who do not have limitations!) are caused by our inability to function effectively in some of the drive states. The ideal of the developed person, therefore, is someone who can function comfortably and be effective in each of his or her drives. Achieving this does not make people superhuman; it makes them well-rounded individuals who are capable of realising their visions. It makes them people who can communicate with others across a wide spectrum because they can relate 'in here' to what is 'out there'. They can engage the appropriate part of their hilltop to connect with different types.

One question we are frequently asked is 'Where does my identity go, where is the real me, if I can be all these things?' As we explained in the Power chapter, the ego is a membrane that separates what a person identifies as 'me' from that which is 'not me'. This happens with possessions, people, knowledge, but it also happens in relation to our drives. We say, 'I am just not that sort of person. I do not identify that particular drive as me.'

Personal development does not mean giving up what we are, it means *expanding* what we are. It means going beyond our self-imposed limitations and opening up our capacities. We say, 'I used to be that, now I am that and this too'. We have all engaged in personal development in our lives, there is no mystique to it. As children we constantly embraced new things, added to our store of abilities, knowledge and awareness. True, we did give up some things. Some things we grew out of, some we were forced out of, others we actively dismissed as belonging to an earlier age – they became 'not me'.

The difficulty we seem to have as adults is that development ceases to be a natural process, and unless we pay conscious attention to it, we stop growing. Most of us stop developing physically in our late teens or early twenties. We suspect that, without effort, psychological growth stops soon after. We settle into what we are, our identity becomes frozen to a greater or lesser degree, and we become the kind of person who can do this but not that, who values this but not that, and who gains satisfaction from this and not that.

We become constrained by the maps we have created – maps about who we are, what we value, what we like and what we are capable of. Personal development means making a conscious effort to redraw the maps. We are not suggesting that we have to abandon our values and belief systems, but expand them. It may mean filling in some features in an area of our map that we have not visited for a long time, adding a new leaf to it or finding appropriate guides to help us explore unfamiliar terrain.

Personal development is a process of consciously modifying our own hilltops. Working with this book has started that process. If you continue to use 7P as a map and 3LT as a spyglass, your map of people, both yourself and others, will change. You will begin to see drives operating clearly in behaviour and attitudes and to recognise your reactions to them. Finding out who you are is the beginning of personal development.

The possibilities for developing any of the drive states are endless. They are all, however, based on one simple observation: *whatever we nourish grows.*

There are people we meet whose predominant drive shines like a beacon through almost everything they do. This is the one they have nourished the most, exercised the most often, and paid most attention to. It has become the one that brings them most rewards, the one they feel comfortable with and therefore the one they continue to engage. It is analogous to fledglings in a nest competing for nourishment – even the slightest advantage leads one to get more food than the others, to grow quickest, to become the strongest and, in turn, to get more food and thereby reinforce the dominance.

Each of us has drives that we have nourished, drives that we have only fed occasionally, and some that we may have actively starved. If you want to develop any of your drives, the basic process is to expose yourself to activities that will nourish them. Below are some examples.

Product drive nourishment

If you want to nourish your Product drive, the focus is physical activity. It can be aimed at health, fitness, strength or stamina: running, gym workouts, strenuous sport, digging, or working with your body as the primary tool. It must demand exertion – your body needs to feel it has been working. Many of us abuse our bodies. We feed them badly, fill them with alcohol, exercise them little, and lose touch with them. Sustained nurturing of your physical being will change not only your shape but also your self-image. You will become a person who can engage this drive as part of your attributes, another facet of your hilltop.

People drive nourishment

The focus for nourishing your People drive is social activity in all its forms. Go to social events; put energy into getting to know people, show interest in what they do. Engage in conversation, be prepared to chat. Make the effort to exchange a few words with people you meet – taxi drivers, shop assistants, etc. Show concern for other people's lives: get involved in an ongoing group that has a shared activity. Many of us find small-talk difficult, pointless or boring, but consciously putting effort into such activities will tap into and develop your own sociability.

Process drive nourishment

If you want to nourish your Process drive the focus can be intellectual stimulation. Commit yourself to a course of study, or research something that interests you. Explore, analyse, and sharpen your intellectual faculties. Open up to new experiences: go to fringe events, explore the unknown, read unusual material, gain exposure to very different perspectives from your own.

Another focus can be self-expression. Engage in debate with Process types on contentious issues, express opinions and back them up with argument. Join a local drama, dance or singing workshop. Many of us avoid intellectual pursuits or being different. We do not feel comfortable in quick-witted situations and we prefer what is familiar to what is unknown. Putting effort into this drive will develop your adaptability and intellectual abilities.

Power drive nourishment

If you want to nourish your Power drive the focus is on developing confidence and self-assertion. Find a good assertiveness programme and enrol in a session. Learn to say what you want, learn to say no. We often lack access to our own Power drive because of a lack of self-worth. Learn to value who you are. Find ways of achieving success, no matter how insignificant it may seem. Develop situations in which you can explore the competitive element, find the urge to win. Introduce some small risks into what you do – nothing at first that would have dire consequences, but a bit of uncertainty. Many of us live very safe lives, based on 'nothing ventured, nothing lost'. Growing confidence and self-esteem is one of the most difficult things for people who have little access to this drive. It is a deeply emotional area with roots in our earliest years.

There are no easy answers. Many people seek some form of counselling or therapy to help them into positively expressing their Power drive. There are many different approaches used in group work that release powerful emotions – be sure to choose judiciously if that is a route you wish to explore.

Plans drive nourishment

If you want to nourish your Plans drive the focus is on organising and conceptualising things. For any task you have to undertake – a work project, a holiday, or whatever – sit down with a pen and paper and spend time planning. Think things through before committing yourself to action. Use Vision to Action as a way of checklisting the issues that need to be addressed. Many of us create unnecessary difficulties for ourselves because of a reluctance or inability to prepare in advance. Take the lead occasionally in organising an activity that you usually leave to someone else. Spend time reading books that offer conceptual structures for understanding anything you are interested in. This, for example, is a book offering a conceptual map of human drives. There are others for understanding organisations, economics, politics and many other social and natural phenomena. By doing this you will build up not only a store of knowledge, but an ability to understand conceptual ideas.

Positioning drive nourishment

If you want to nourish your Positioning drive the focus is sensitivity and appreciation. Our literature, music and art abound with expressions of meaning. Read literature that captures the spirit, that focuses on the deeper expressions of humanity. Immerse yourself in books that are essentially spiritual in nature – those that pose the question of the meaning of life and our relationship to the larger picture. Learn to view everything as in some way connected with everything else: the natural world, events both large and small, movements in society, things that happen within your social group.

Work at developing close communication with at least one other person. Learn to share your softer, more vulnerable aspect. The personal growth movement has an almost endless supply of courses and programmes aimed at putting people in touch with their deeper nature – find one that might interest you. In the hectic society that many of us live and work in, sensitivity can be easily abandoned. It often means finding the time to be still, to engage in a meditative process of whatever kind, to make a space where you can simply 'be'.

Purpose drive nourishment

If you want to nourish your Purpose drive the focus is creativity and imagination. Get involved in some kind of artistic endeavour. Join an art class or creative music programme. Open the channels that start to stir the creative elements within you. Find something, no matter how small, that you want to create and set about doing it. Many of us feel that we are not creative because creativity is the domain of a few exceptional people. We are limited by our own images that say this to us. We do not have to be world-beaters to manifest a creative act – making a pair of earrings can qualify. Creativity appears as the bounds of the possible are broken. Read literature that stretches the bounds of what you consider possible. It might be on the scientific frontier or the frontiers of human endeavour – there are many stories of people who have achieved the impossible or fought against limitations or oppression to fulfil their goals.

Remember, whatever we nourish grows. Whatever we put effort into will develop us. The questions only you can answer are:

- Do I want to?
- Can I find the commitment?
- Which drives do I want to develop?
- How will I go about it?

Personal development is not easy. It does take effort. If it were easy we would have already done it. However, being hard work does not mean that it is not enjoyable. We are not suggesting that you commit yourself to taking nasty medicine simply because it is good for you. Working on developing any of your drive states can – and should – be enjoyable, certainly after the initial inertia has been overcome. If it does not become enjoyable, then you will need to look afresh at the activity and your underlying motivations.

Communication with other, different hilltops

Communicating with others demands that we communicate with ourselves.

Communicating with people who are very different from us can be difficult – it can stretch us. To do so successfully demands that we expand our access to the drives within us and grow in our ability to see things through unfamiliar eyes.

By developing ourselves we can communicate with others, and by communicating with others we can develop ourselves.

There are no better teachers of communication than the people you want to communicate with. If you want to learn what a certain drive is about, talk to those who are driven by it. Use 3LT, ask questions, listen, find out, understand.

If you are prepared to put aside your perspective temporarily and really learn to enter another person's inner world, you will, at the same time, be opening up pathways into your own. What this demands is that you develop the ability to stand as much as possible on another's hilltop, look out and see the world from that perspective, and be able to value and agree with it as a real and valid point of view. From the place you normally occupy, you may have a different perspective, and disagree with the other person. But, as already mentioned, you will not communicate from there. Entering another's inner world develops rapport, credibility and trust which lays the foundation for achieving true communication.

Summary

- Self-development and self-fulfilment go hand in hand.
- Self-development can focus on our predominant *and* our least dominant drives.
- Our limitations are based on our inability to function in certain drive states.
- Personal development means expanding, not giving up, who we are.
- What we nourish grows.
- Each of the 7Ps of drive can be nourished with specific activities that promote growth.
- While personal development may not be easy, it can and should be enjoyable.
- By developing ourselves we can communicate with others.
- By communicating with others we can develop ourselves.

Afterword

Human beings are complex creatures. In this book we have attempted to restrict ourselves to examining the role of drives in shaping our perceptions and behaviour. Yet within this there is still more we could cover. We acknowledge, for instance, that for the sake of clarity we have dealt with types of people who have a single drive as their predominance. While there are many of us who fit this model, there are many others who have multiple predominances, those who have equal access to two, three or more of their drives.

We have introduced you to the 7P model as a way of understanding something of who you are, and why people do some of the things they do. It is our best attempt to date to produce a useful and enlightening map for understanding a very complex topology. If you continue to explore yourself and others, using the Three Level Technique (3LT), you will discover much more detail than we could ever describe here.

We need to stress again that the 7Ps of drive is not an attempt to box people in and reduce them to stereotypes, but a way of understanding what we find when we explore anyone's hilltop. In some instances you will be unclear about where certain behaviours might fit, or be tempted to squeeze them into a box to make them fit. If it comes to a choice between labelling a person's drives or understanding the person, we would suggest that you always work with the in-depth understanding rather than focusing on where it might fit. The map is to help you understand people, not the other way round.

The benefit of working to understand people, to communicate with them better, is that you actually begin to appreciate and respect the qualities of people whom you might previously have dismissed. You begin to accept and like them for who they are, not simply because their hilltop is close to yours. Consequently, it becomes easier to work alongside them and value what they have to offer.

Ultimately, the same holds true for ourselves. As we said, we can be our own worst judges. If we can accept others we can accept ourselves. We hope this book has been of some value in finding out who you are, for, without that understanding, acceptance can be difficult. If you can accept all of you, your strengths and current limitations, then you have laid the foundation for successfully getting to where you want to be. We wish you success.

Quarto Consulting Notes

Roy Calvert, Brian Durkin, Eugenio Grandi and Kevin Martin came together in 1985 as founding partners of Quarto. Quarto is an organisation development and training consultancy helping client organisations to operate more effectively in times of increasing complexity and rapid change. This book is based on their first book, *First Find Your Hilltop*, and is published in celebration of nearly two decades of work.

There are many people who in various ways contributed to this book. Whether as colleagues, clients, participants in training or overtly as the authors' teachers, they have all offered opportunities to learn, extend and develop ideas. For this, the authors especially want to thank Eddie Gallagher, David Hodgkinson, Kevin Kingsland, Eric Mitchell, Stuart Smith, John Kay and Bob Griffiths. These people deserve a special mention for their inspiration, encouragement and willingness to work with the authors over the years.

Quarto's primary concern has been to help organisations generate and implement development strategies that serve the needs of the business. A major element of this work involves unlocking the potential within the organisation's most important resource, its people. Quarto works with individuals and teams to develop the knowledge, skills and awareness necessary for them to be fully effective in their roles.

Quarto also offers publicly available personal development programmes based on the ideas presented in this book. For further information contact:

Quarto
4 The Square
Aspley Guise
Bedfordshire MK17 8DF
United Kingdom
Tel +44-1908-281-030
Fax +44-1908-281-030
quarto@quartoconsulting.co.uk
www.quartoconsulting.com

Index

Ability and skill level 175
Abstractions 103-5, 115
Academia 77
Acceptance 61
Accounting 106
Acquisition 98, 102
Action 47
Action stages 157
Adaptability 74
Administration 115
Advertising 116, 137
Appearance 45, 53, 57, 59
Army 107
Art 124, 127, 129, 139, 141
Assertiveness 65
Athletics, see Sport
Attitudes 47, 131
Attract and retain talent 8, 122
Authority 103, 107-08, 111, 113-14

Balance 34, 116-17, 130, 146
Behaviour 35-6, 41-45, 75, 134, 143,
    147, 150, 155
Beliefs 16, 18-19, 25, 109, 125
Belonging, sense of 61-63, 66-70
Blind Men and Elephant Story 23
Branding 116
Broadcasting 21-22, 27, 32, 143, 165
Budget 106

Careers 90, 122
    Changing 173-78
Caring professions 62
Catalyst 121

Challenge 24, 87, 89-90, 102
Change 9, 24, 33, 74-81, 85, 109-10,
    113, 121, 129, 135, 140-41, 152-63,
    173-78
    Through communication 9, 164-72
    Through personal development
    179-85
Changing jobs and careers 173-78
Choice 13, 33
Civil service 107
Collector 79-80, 99, 111, 115
Commitment 83, 87, 94-96, 102, 153-
    54, 158, 160, 163, 165-70, 172, 184
Committee 112
Common sense 84-85
Communication 12, 22, 37, 97, 120-21,
    123, 164-72; see also Change
    through communication
Community spirit 81
Competition 87, 90, 102
Compliance vs. commitment 165
Computer technologies 137
Conceptual work 49, 103, 115
Conformity, conventionality 61, 66,
    69, 71-73, 112
Connection 117
Context 116, 159, 167
Counsellor 120, 129
Crafts, handicrafts 124
'Creatives' 77, 137, 142
Creativity 131, 137, 142, 157
Culture of organisations 121, 176
Customer care 61

Decision-making 9, 66, 93-96, 106-07, 160

Depth 116-17

Design 137

Dexterity 64

Discovery tool 35, 38, 41

Dislike people 147-49

Drive profile, personal 12, 29-30, 32-35, 42-45, 58, 73, 151-52, 163

Drives 10, 12, 15, 26-27, 33, 35, 42-44, 143, 148, 173
  Demanded by job 145
  Competition of 30, 34
  Hierarchy of 29
  Satisfaction of 30, 34, 143

Ego 88-89, 101-02, 123

Emotional attachment 87, 89, 94

Empowerment 33

Energy 93-95, 160-61

Enjoyment, see Fulfilment

Entertainment 56, 70, 77-78

Entrepreneurism 95-97, 102, 123

Environmentalism intro, 117-18, 121, 123-26, 130

Envisioning, see Vision, Imagination

Facts 37-41

Feedback 10, 44, 149-51

Finance 106

Fitness 45, 51-53, 60

Food 55, 60

Friendship 61, 66-67, 73

Fulfilment 8, 12-16, 143, 146, 155, 157, 173, 176

Future 104, 122, 135

Games 110-111

Getting what you want, see Influencing

Graphics 120

Greening, see Environmentalism

Harmony 116-17, 120, 126, 128-30

Hawthorne studies 62

Health 45, 55-57, 59, 81

Hilltops 12, 13-28, 33, 35-36, 38, 46-48, 58-59, 61-62, 66, 71, 73, 75, 88-89, 91-92, 103, 120-21, 128, 131, 143, 147-49, 152, 154, 164-65, 167, 170, 178, 181

Honesty, 38, 41, 44

Humour 13, 73, 84

Identity 87-89

Image 119, 132, 135-36, 140-42, 158, 166, 172, 174-75

Imagination 13134, 137-40

Importance 37-41

Individuality 15-17, 82

Influencing 7, 12, 26, 90, 101, 153, 164-72
  As process 166-72

Information processing 103

Information technology (IT) 30, 75

Information, levels of 37-41

Information, quality, see Quality of information

Inspiration 131, 135, 142

Integration 116, 120, 128-30

Intellectual stimulation 74-77, 82, 84

Intelligence 48-49

Interpretation, see Perception

Interviews 22, 176-78

Intimacy 116-17, 127-28

Intuition 116, 119, 130

Invention 136-37, 142

Jobs or careers, changing 173-78
Judgments 19-25, 31, 35, 38-39, 58-59, 150; see also Values

Know who you are 9

Labelling 44, 108
Law, legal system, legislation 105-06
Leader 95
Leisure interests 12, 45, 146, 151
    People drive 67-68
    Plans drive 110-11
    Positioning drive 125
    Power drive 98
    Process drive 78
    Product drive 50-51
    Purpose drive 139
Like and dislike, see Judgement
Limitations 156, 163, 180
    People drive 64-65
    Plans drive 106-07
    Positioning drive 122-23
    Power drive 96
    Process drive 78
    Product drive 49
    Purpose drive 138
Listening 27, 35-44, 96, 123, 165, 171, 184

Male occupations, traditional 46-47
Management 18, 26-27, 93, 95, 97, 102, 106
Manual work 45-46
Map 11, 103, 110, 131, 147, 180-81
Market research 118
Marketing 116, 119, 130
Maslow, Abraham 29, 45
Meaning 19, 35, 37-41, 116-18, 123, 125, 128-29
Membrane, ego as 31, 66, 87-89, 92, 180
Messenger and message 39-41
Mirror 148-49
Mission 131, 133-34, 142
Motivation 9-11, 27, 35, 37-38, 143

Naisbitt, John 8, 118
Needs 10, 29, 45, 122, 173
Negative aspects
    People drive 71
    Plans drive 113
    Positioning drive 128
    Power drive 100
    Process drive 84
    Product drive 57
    Purpose drive 140
New ideas 75
Nourishing
    People drive 181
    Plans drive 182-83
    Positioning drive 183
    Power drive 182
    Process drive 182
    Product drive 181
    Purpose drive 183-84
Nursing 62

Office work 63
Opinion, see Judgements
Order 103-04, 114
Organising 29, 103, 106, 115, 160; see also Planning

Peace 116-17, 128
People drive 61-73, 117, 127, 152, 171
Perception 20-21, 25, 47, 147-149

Permission points 39

Persistence 162

Personal awareness 10-12, 24, 33, 35-6, 42-44

Personal development, change through 124, 179-85

Personal drives profile, see Drives, personal profile

Perspective, see Hilltops

Peters, Tom 134

Physical activity, experience, problems, prowess 45-50, 52, 54, 60, 74

Planning 47-49, 65-66, 97, 104,114,119

Plans Drive 103-06, 119, 131, 135, 170

Policy 106, 108

Positioning Drive 116-30

Power Drive 87-102, 104, 123, 131, 152, 168, 170

Pragmatism 47-48, 60

Precision 105, 115

Predominant drives or styles 9, 32, 42-44, 47, 75, 179

Prejudice 71

Principles 109, 115

Problem-solving 48, 131, 138-39, 142

Process Drive 74-86, 103, 105, 117, 124, 131, 171

Process of change, see Change as process

Product Drive 45-60, 171

Projects 76

Purpose Drive 131-42, 155

Qualifications 108

Quality circles 48

Quality of information 27, 37-44, 168

Questioning 35-41

Rationality 103, 109, 115

Recognition 53, 87, 91-92, 100, 116

Relationships 82, 116, 162, 167-72

Relationships, building with different types 167-68

Religion and spirituality 109, 126-28

Research 74-76, 86, 105, 137

Responsibility, see Taking responsibility

Retail trade 62, 102

Reward early, 123

Risk 107, 160

Role, role perception 18, 45-47, 96, 122

Routine 76

Rules 107, 114-115

Science 105, 136

Security
  People drive 69-70
  Plans drive 108
  Positioning drive 127
  Power drive 99-100
  Process drive 81-82
  Product drive 52

Self-awareness, see Personal awareness

Self-development 33, 179-85

Self-discovery, see Personal awareness

Self-esteem 87, 92, 100

Self-expression 77-80

Self-fulfilment 179

Selfishness 89, 92-93, 101, 123

Self-limitations 32

Selling 90, 102

Sensitivity 116-18, 128

Sequence 161

Service 102

Seven Ps (7Ps)
  And change 157-62
  And commitments of others 169
  And influencing 166-67
Seven Ps of Drive (7Ps) 12, 26-34, 42-
  44, 147, 157, 163; see also People,
  Plans, Positioning, Power, Process,
  Product, Purpose Drives
Sex 45, 54, 57, 60
Sexism 54
Social welfare 123
Socialising 67-68, 73-74, 81
Sport 45, 50-51, 58
Spotting drives 32, 37
Status
  Plans drive 107-08
  Power drive 91-92
  Process drive 83-84
  Product drive 53-54
  Purpose drive 137-38
Status quo 103, 110, 112, 114
Stereotyping 31
Structure 103-04, 108, 114
Success 87, 90, 94, 99-102, 169
Systems 115

Taking responsibility 147, 172, 176
Team spirit 62-63, 73
Theory 114
Thoroughness 105, 107, 115

Three Level Technique (3LT) 12, 35-
  41, 43, 143, 147, 151, 155, 163, 171,
  181, 184
Tradition 103, 112, 115
Travel 79-80, 82
Trend, 118-19, 122, 130
Trust 150, 167
Types, typology, notion of re: 7 Ps 31,
  36, 43, 48, 143, 154

Unconventionality 74, 78, 86
Understanding others 9-12, 14-17, 20,
  26, 34-35, 42-44
Understanding ourselves, see Personal awareness

Values 18, 20-21, 25-27, 31, 37-38, 42,
  47, 53, 131, 143, 148-50, 177-78, 180
Variety 76
Violence 52, 58-59
Vision 131-34, 136, 140-41, 157, 158,
  178
Vision to Action 12, 152-64, 166, 172
Vision to Action, blocks to re: 7Ps 158-
  62

Work, match with Drive 24, 59-60, 72,
  85-86, 101-02, 114-15, 129, 141
World view, see Hilltops